INSTANT [illegible] MAKE AND DO

KATIE THOMPSON

Kevin Mayhew

First published in 1996 by
KEVIN MAYHEW LTD
Rattlesden
Bury St Edmunds
Suffolk IP30 0SZ

ISBN 0 86209 790 8
Catalogue No 1396042

Front cover: Claire James

Edited by Peter Dainty and Stephen Haddelsey
Cover design by Graham Johnstone and Veronica Ward
Typesetting by Louise Hill
Printed and bound in Great Britain.

Contents

The secret of happiness

Reading

(cf Matthew 5:1-12)

One day when Jesus was being followed by a large crowd, he climbed a hillside, sat down,and began to speak:

'Happy are gentle people,
for they shall be treated with gentleness.
Happy are people who forgive others,
for they shall be forgiven.
Happy are the poor for they shall see Heaven.
Happy are people who do what is right
and care about others.
Happy are people who make peace
and bring friendship.
Be happy even if people are unkind
and say nasty things to you
because you believe in me,
for you will have great rewards in Heaven.'

Discussion

Imagine if you could have anything you wanted to make you feel happy, what would you choose?

Would such feelings of happiness last forever?

Jesus wanted to give us some 'guidelines' to follow which can make us truly happy. This happiness will stay in our hearts forever.

Think of a train rattling along a track. What would happen if the track was broken or suddenly ended?

These guidelines keep us on the 'track' to happiness. Without this 'track' our journey would be much harder, and we might lose our way.

Jesus often used stories called parables to explain what he meant. (Choose one parable to talk about in detail, or give a brief outline of each example and discuss what we learn from them.)

1. Happy are those who do what is right.
   (cf Luke 10:30-35)

One day a man was travelling from Jerusalem to Jericho, when a gang of robbers attacked him. They stole everything he had and after beating him, they left him to die. Two men passed by, but neither stopped. Finally, a man from Samaria found the man lying in the road, and was filled with pity. He bandaged his wounds and gave him a drink, before taking him to the nearest inn where he cared for him.

2. Happy are people who forgive.
   (cf Matthew 18:22-34)

Once there was a king who had many servants. One of these servants owed him a lot of money and could not pay him back.The king was ready to punish him, but the servant begged for mercy, and the king forgave him his debt. Later, this servant met another man who owed him a small amount of money. The man could not pay and asked the servant for mercy. The servant was furious and had him thrown into jail. When the king heard of this, he sent for the servant that he had forgiven. 'You asked me for mercy and I forgave you,' the king said. 'Could you not also be forgiving towards this other man?' The king had his servant thrown into jail until he paid back all that he owed.

Activity

Make a 'Happiness train' with a picture of each child riding on board.

Closing Prayer

Jesus,
you shared the secret
of everlasting happiness with us,
and showed us how to find and keep it.
Help us to live by your 'guidelines'
and to share this happiness with others.

The
Happiness
Train
Forgiveness
Kindness
Peace
makers

Matthew the tax collector

Reading

(cf Matthew 9:9-13)

One day as Jesus was walking along he saw a man called Matthew who was a tax collector. He went over to him and said, 'Follow me.' Matthew did as Jesus told him. They went to Matthew's house where Jesus stayed for supper. Many other tax collectors came and shared the meal with Jesus and his disciples. Jesus overheard a Pharisee asking one of his disciples, 'Why is your master friendly with such dishonest and unkind people?'

Jesus turned to him and said, 'Good people do not need my help. It is people such as these tax collectors who need me; I will forgive them and call them to follow me.'

Discussion

Tax collectors were hated by the Jews, do you know why?

The people had to give a part of any money they earned to the Roman government in taxes. People like Matthew collected the taxes from the people, and often charged them extra money which they kept for themselves. The Jews hated them because they worked for the Romans and were often dishonest.

When Jesus asked Matthew to become a follower, do you think everyone was surprised?

Matthew was greedy and selfish, ready to cheat and take their money. Everyone was amazed that Jesus wanted to befriend this man.

What did the Pharisees say?

Pharisees were Jews who strictly obeyed the Jewish law and were proud of their goodness. They disapproved because Jesus chose to befriend a sinner rather than one of them.

Matthew was not a good man, but are any of us good all the time?

Just because we are not good all the time, Jesus does not stop being our friend. He wanted us to see people like Matthew with God's loving eyes. Not to judge them and to turn away, but to reach out and forgive them.

Do you think that meeting Jesus changed Matthew's life?

Jesus changed the lives of everyone he met. His love and goodness spread to those around him, and they in turn shared it with others. When Matthew followed Jesus that day, his life changed direction as he walked in the footsteps of Jesus, and he realised how selfish and dishonest he had been. Jesus was willing to offer forgiveness and friendship so that Matthew could make a fresh start in life! Matthew had a change of heart.

Activity

Cut out the figure of Matthew and a set of clothes with which to 'dress' him. These can be coloured and decorated as befits a wealthy man. Stick several bags of gold to a belt on his waist. After colouring, stick the heart shape onto his chest, to show that Matthew had a change of heart.

Closing Prayer

Dear Jesus,
you were ready to forgive Matthew
and offer him your friendship,
just as your heavenly Father
is always ready to forgive us
and let us make a fresh start.
Help us always to remember this,
so that we are ready to forgive
those we meet on our journey through life.

Gold
Gold
Gold
Gold

The wheat and the weeds

Reading

(cf Matthew 13:24-30, 36-43)

Jesus told the people another parable:

'One day a farmer sowed his field with wheat, but that night as he slept, his enemy crept into the field and scattered weed seeds amongst the wheat.

'Days passed and as the wheat sprouted and grew, so did the weeds, and the farmer realised what his enemy had done. One of the farm workers asked him, "Master, do you want us to pull up the weeds?" But the farmer answered, "No, let them grow together until harvest time, because if you pull up the weeds now you might pull up the wheat too! When the harvest comes, the harvesters can separate the wheat from the weeds. Then I can store the wheat in my barn, and burn the weeds."'

When the disciples asked Jesus to explain the story he said: 'I am the man who sowed the wheat, and the devil is my enemy who scattered the weeds. The wheat seeds are the people who hear my word and follow me, and the weeds are the wicked people who will not listen to me. The end of the world will be like harvest time, when good and bad people will be separated by angels sent by God. The good people will share God's glory and happiness in heaven, but the wicked people will be punished and will never see God.'

Discussion

Do you know how the farmers sowed their seeds in those days?

They scattered them from a large open basket.

In today's parable, what happened to the farmer's field of wheat?

Why does no one like weeds?

Weeds stop the other plants from growing tall and strong. They choke them with their roots and block out the sunlight with their leaves.

Why did the farmer not want his workers to pull out the weeds?

He did not want to risk losing any of the good seed. Like the wheat and weeds, God allows good and bad people to live side by side. Goodness and love are strong and God wants to allow wicked people a chance to change their ways before the end of time.

Can you think of any examples of people who changed their way of life after they had met Jesus?

Remember Matthew the tax collector, who gave up everything to follow Jesus, and Zacchaeus the dishonest tax collector who made a fresh start after Jesus had forgiven him.

What did Jesus promise for good and bad people at the end of the world?

By the life we lead on earth, we can choose to be like the wheat, stored safely in the farmer's barn, and live with God forever in heaven, or we can be like the weeds, burned at harvest time, and never be with God.

Activity

Colour the bundles of wheat and weeds. Untangle the maze to show what happens to them.

Closing Prayer

Jesus, show us the way to eternal life.
Walk beside us on our journey,
until your angels lead us
to share your everlasting happiness at the end of time.

God's Kingdom
God's Kingdom

THE MIRACLE OF THE LOAVES AND FISH

READING

(cf Matthew 14:13-21)

A large crowd had followed Jesus to a hillside beside the Sea of Galilee, to hear him teaching. As it grew late in the day the disciples asked Jesus to send the people away to find some food for themselves. 'They do not need to leave,' said Jesus, 'we can share our food with them.'

'But all we have for ourselves are five loaves and two fish, and there must be five thousand people to feed!' exclaimed the disciples. 'Bring the food to me,' said Jesus and he told the crowds to sit down quietly. Jesus took the loaves and fish and gave thanks to God. He blessed the bread, broke it, and handed it to the disciples to share with the people. There was plenty for everyone to eat, and when they had finished eating, they filled twelve baskets with the scraps. The people were amazed and they went away telling everyone about the miracle they had seen that day.

DISCUSSION

Why were the disciples surprised when Jesus told them to share their food with the crowd?

They only had five loaves and two fish, so how could they possibly feed so many? Jesus shows us that we must be ready to share whatever we have with others.

Have you any idea how big a crowd of five thousand people is?

Compare the size of your Sunday congregation or the local school, something familiar to the children so they appreciate how many people needed to be fed.

What did Jesus do with the loaves of bread?

He blessed them according to the Jewish custom, broke them and gave them out to the disciples.

Can you remember another occasion when Jesus blessed bread and shared it with other people?

The Last Supper.

How do we remember this meal?

When we have Holy Communion. Just as Jesus fed the thousands that day, so he continues to feed millions today through the bread and wine of Holy Communion.

How do you think the disciples felt as they gave out the loaves and the fish?

They had seen Jesus perform many wonderful miracles, and they believed in him. However, this did not stop them being amazed by the power of Jesus, as he again proved to them that he was indeed the Son of God.

ACTIVITY

Use small squares of ready gummed paper for the children to stick over the shapes to make a mosaic picture. You may like to show a copy of the famous Byzantine mosaic of the loaves and fishes found at Tabgha where this miracle is said to have taken place.

CLOSING PRAYER

Jesus,
help us to share whatever we have with other,
and not to be greedy in any way.
As we remember our brothers and sisters
in other countries
who have no food,
we pray that the rest of the world
will learn to share too,
so that the world can be a happier place.

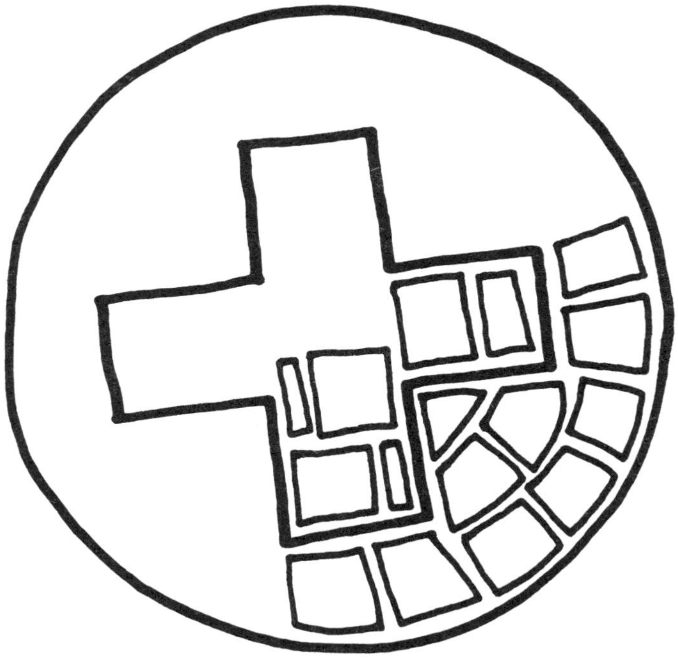

Have faith

Reading

(cf Matthew 14:22-33)

Before going up to the hills to pray alone, Jesus told his disciples to sail to the other side of the lake. As night fell, the wind grew stronger and the disciples' boat was tossed about by the waves. Suddenly they saw someone coming towards the boat, walking on the water, and they were terrified, because they thought it was a ghost! But Jesus called to them, 'Don't be afraid, it's me!'

Peter shouted to Jesus, 'Lord, if that really is you, tell me to come to you across the water.'

'Come!' said Jesus.

So Peter climbed out of the boat and lowered himself onto the water. Looking straight at Jesus, he began to walk towards him, but as he moved further from the boat and felt the strength of the wind, he grew afraid. Suddenly he began to sink and he cried out, 'Save me, Jesus!' As Jesus reached out his hand and pulled Peter to safety he said, 'Why did you not trust me Peter? Is your belief so weak?' When they got back to the boat, the other disciples knelt before Jesus and said, 'You are truly the Son of God.'

Discussion

At first, what did the disciples think they had seen coming across the water towards them?

A ghost.

What did they do?

Imagine how frightened they must have been to suddenly see someone walking on top of the water towards them on a dark stormy night. They probably cried out in fear and tried to hide somewhere on the boat.

What did Jesus do to calm their fears?

He said, 'Do not be afraid.' Jesus said this on several other occasions when the disciples were frightened by some of the amazing things they saw. Remember when he appeared to them in the upper room after his death, and again said, 'Do not be afraid.'

What did Peter do when he heard Jesus calling him to come?

Peter climbed out of the boat and began to walk towards Jesus!

Can an ordinary person normally walk on water?

We can swim in water and we can lie and float in the water, but if we try to stand without anything to make us float we only sink.

What was so special about Peter that allowed him to walk on the water towards Jesus?

Peter was full of courage and faith. He was the first one to realise that Jesus was truly the Son of God.

What happened to Peter when he felt the strength of the wind?

He began to sink beneath the waves, because for just a moment his faith and belief weakened and he felt afraid. Sometimes we are like Peter, full of courage and enthusiasm at first, but often let down by our lack of faith and by fear of the unknown.

What did Jesus do?

Peter was an ordinary person like us, and he would often let Jesus down because his faith was weak. (Remember how he denied Jesus three times after his arrest.) Jesus is always forgiving and ready to reach out his hand to save us just as he reached out that night and saved Peter on the lake.

Activity

Use squares of coloured paper to make boats with masts and sails.

Closing Prayer

Lord, give us the courage and faith of Peter,
whose belief was so strong
that he could walk towards Jesus across the lake.
In times of weakness,
reach out your hand to us
and rescue us from our doubts.

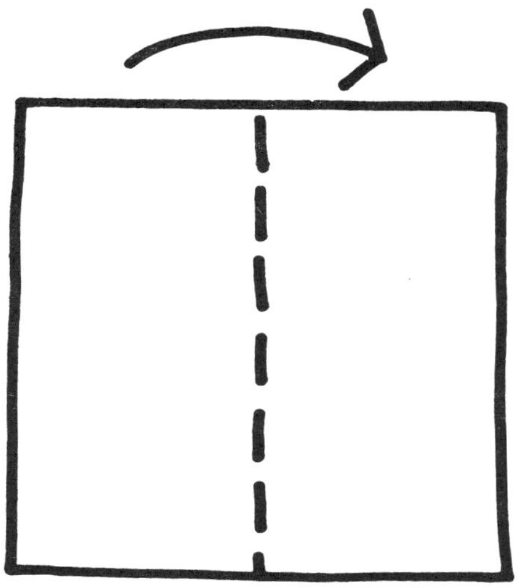

1. Fold square of paper in half.

2. Fold edge of paper back to meet folded edge.

3. Turn paper over and repeat action. Then unfold paper.

4. Fold corners into middle crease.

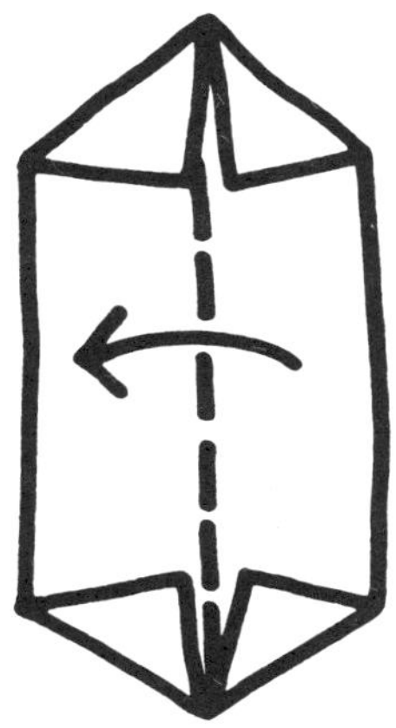

5. Fold right edge over to folded edge.

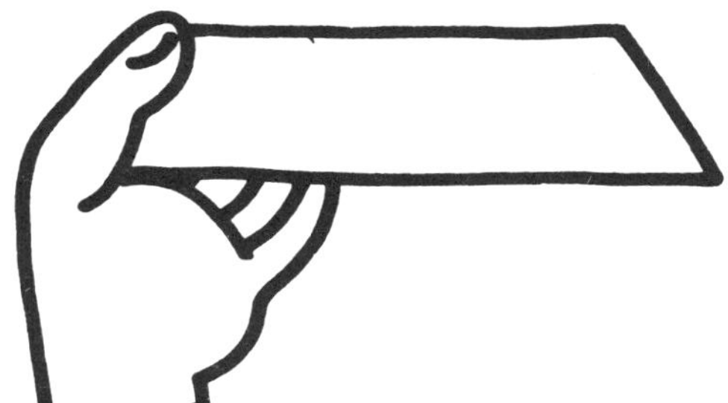

6. Put fingers inside and push corners down with thumbs to make boat 'stand'.

7.

8.

GOD'S WAY

READING

(cf Matthew 16:21-26)

Jesus began to tell his disciples that he would be brought before the high priests, and be put to death before rising to life again.

'Lord, this cannot be allowed to happen!' exclaimed Peter, who was deeply upset by what Jesus had told them.

But Jesus said, 'Peter, your way is not God's way. If you follow me, sometimes things will be difficult, but you must accept them and try not to take the easy way out.'

DISCUSSION

What made Peter feel so upset?

Jesus had told the disciples that he was going to die.

What did Peter want Jesus to do?

Peter knew that if they kept out of harm's way Jesus would be safe, and could not be put to death. He did not want Jesus to go to Jerusalem for the Passover celebration.

Jesus said to Peter, 'Your way is not God's way.' What do you think he meant?

Peter wanted to take the easy way out because he did not want Jesus to suffer and die. Jesus chose to follow God's way; to give up his life so that God could save all of us. Jesus had been sent by God the Father to suffer and die and bring everlasting life to the world. He showed how much he really loved us by following God's way. Like Peter, sometimes we do not fully understand God's way of doing things, but we should trust our Father as Jesus did.

When we find it difficult trying to live as Jesus taught us, should we give up easily?

As Jesus prayed in the Garden of Gethsemane he felt afraid to die. He did not run away and hide, but instead he asked God to give him the courage to do what he knew was right. With the help of Jesus, we too can face up to any difficulties in our lives and choose to show God how much *we* love *Him*, by following his way.

ACTIVITY

Photocopy and cut out the bookmark templates to be coloured by the children.

CLOSING PRAYER

Lord,
we pray for people who are suffering difficulties;
the homeless and unemployed;
the sick and the lonely;
the hungry and the poor.
Share your courage and strength with them
and surround them with your love.

God's
Follow God's way Follow
Way Follow God's way

God's
Follow God's way Follow
Way Follow God's way

God's
Follow God's way Follow
Way Follow God's way

God's glory on the mountain

Reading

(cf Matthew 17:1-9)

One day Jesus asked Peter, James and John to come and pray with him. He led them to the top of a steep mountain, where it was peaceful and quiet, and they could be alone. Jesus began to pray to his heavenly Father when suddenly he appeared to change! His face and clothes shone with a brilliant light, as dazzling as the rays of the sun. Then the disciples saw Moses and Elijah on either side of Jesus, talking to him. Peter jumped up with excitement and said, 'Lord, this is wonderful! I could make three shelters – one for each of you!' At that moment a cloud streaming with light appeared above them, and a voice said, 'This is my Son, whom I love very much. Listen to what he says.' The disciples were so terrified that they threw themselves to the ground and hid their faces. Then Jesus said gently, 'Get up my friends, do not be afraid.' When they looked up, Jesus was standing alone. As they came down the mountain together, Jesus told them firmly, 'You must not tell anyone about what you have seen today, until the Son of God has risen from the dead.'

Discussion

Jesus led his friends to a mountain top. In the Old Testament, mountains were often the place where God appeared to people.

When Jesus began to pray, what happened?

How did he change?

Two people appeared beside Jesus – can you remember their names?

Moses was the man chosen by God to lead his people out of slavery in Egypt, to the Promised Land. He had taken them through the Red Sea and across the desert for forty long years. He collected the Ten Commandments on Mount Sinai. Elijah was a 'prophet', a man who spoke for God. He had warned people not to disobey God and to follow his rules. Like Moses he always trusted God and did whatever He asked.

The disciples were amazed at this sight, but what happened next to make them fall to the ground in fear?

God wanted the three friends to know that Jesus was His Son. In days to come, when Jesus would suffer and die, they would remember the glory of God that they had seen on the mountain that day. He was showing himself as they would know him in heaven.

Activity

Cut out and colour in these figures to create a 'Transfiguration scene'.

Closing Prayer

Dear God, Peter, James and John
saw the light of your glory
shining from Jesus
on the mountain that day.
Jesus shares that light
and his love with all of us.
May the light in our hearts
help us to 'change'
so that we will be more like Jesus;
filled with his joy,
happiness and goodness.

Be forgiving

Reading

(cf Matthew 18:23-35)

One day Jesus said, 'There was once a king who had many servants. One servant owed the king a great deal of money, but he had nothing to pay him with. "I will sell you and your family as slaves, and use the money to pay for your debts," said the king.

'The servant fell to his knees and begged for another chance. "Somehow I will repay everything I owe," he pleaded. The king was a kind and generous man and, taking pity on the servant, cancelled his debts and let him go.

'Later that day, the servant met another man who owed him a small amount of money. When he could not pay what he owed, the servant had him thrown into jail.

'When the news reached the king, he sent for the unforgiving servant.

'"Could you not forgive someone just as I forgave you?" he asked. Then he had the servant thrown into prison until he could pay back all that he owed the king.' Jesus said, 'Just as my Father forgives you, so you must be ready to forgive others with all your heart.'

Discussion

Why was the servant in trouble with the king?

At first what did the king do?

He said he would sell the servant and his family as slaves to pay off his debts.

What did he do instead?

Even though the servant owed him a great deal of money, he completely forgave his debt and gave him the chance to make a fresh start.

Did the servant show the same forgiveness towards the man who owed him some money?

He quickly forgot the good example shown by the king and what a difference the king's mercy had made to his life.

What happened to the unforgiving servant?

The angry king had him thrown into jail until he could repay all that he owed.

What message does Jesus give us in this parable?

That we must be ready to forgive others, however large or small their wrongdoing, if we want to be forgiven ourselves.

God will always forgive us but in the same way he expects us to show mercy to others.

Activity

Photocopy the series of pictures telling today's parable. After colouring, pin them on a board for the children to look at and discuss.

Closing Prayer

Jesus taught us a prayer that mentions how we must forgive others when we ask forgivenss ourselves. Listen closely to the words that speak of forgiveness:
Our Father . . .

THE UNFORGIVING SERVANT

Making choices

Reading

(cf Matthew 21:28-32)

Jesus told this story to the high priests: 'Once there was a man who had two sons. He said to the older one, "Go and work in the vineyard today," but the son answered, "I will not go because I don't want to." Later the son changed his mind and went to work after all.

'When the man asked his other son to go and work in his vineyard too, he said, "Of course I will go," but he did not do what he said he would.'

Jesus asked the high priests, 'Which of these sons did what their father wanted?'

'The older one of course,' they replied.

Jesus said to them, 'The people you call sinners will enter God's kingdom before any of you, because they listened and believed what John the Baptist told them. You would not listen and believe, and your hearts have not changed.'

Discussion

Did the older son do what his father wanted straight away?

At first he chose to do what *he* wanted and not what he knew was right. Later he felt bad about this choice, had a change of heart and went to work in the vineyard.

What did the second son do?

Although at first he agreed to go and work, he chose to ignore what his father had asked, and do what he wanted instead.

Why did Jesus compare the older son with the people the high priests called sinners?

These people had made bad choices in their lives and done the wrong thing. But they listened to John the Baptist's message, and like the older son they realised that they were wrong. They too had a change of heart and tried to do what was right.

Why were the high priests like the second son?

They heard John the Baptist's message but had not really listened to it. They were not ready to admit that they had made the wrong choices in their lives, or to ask for God's forgiveness. Their hearts were not ready to change and they were not willing to live as Jesus showed them.

What is the message of this parable?

Even if we get things wrong and make foolish choices, God will always give us a second chance to make things right again, if we have a change of heart. By making the right choices in our lives, we will be welcomed into the kingdom of God.

Activity

Give each child a copy of the maze so they can find the way to God's kingdom.

Closing Prayer

Lord, when I choose the way to go,
help me choose the good way.
When I choose the things to say,
help me say what you'd say.
Help me always do what's right;
keep me always in your sight.

The kingdom of God
End
Start
Baptism

The Wedding Party

Reading

(cf Matthew 22:1-14)

One day Jesus said, 'The kingdom of heaven is like this:

A king planned a great party for his son's wedding. When everything was ready, he sent his servants to tell all the guests who had been invited to come and join in the celebrations, but each of them had an excuse for not coming. The king was furious and said to his servants, "These people do not deserve to share in my party, so go out and invite everyone you meet. They can come to the wedding instead!" Soon the hall was filled with people, good and bad alike. The king noticed one man who had not bothered to dress for the occasion. He sent for his servants and the man was thrown out into the dark.'

Discussion

If you want people to come to your birthday party, what do you give or send to them?

What sort of things do you tell them on the invitation?

- the date
- the place
- the time
- what to wear, for example it might be fancy dress or a silly hats party

Imagine if everything was ready for your party – the cake, the games, the bouncy castle, but when you went to collect your guests no-one wanted to come. *How would you feel?*

In the story, what did the king do when no-one who had been invited came to the wedding celebration?

He invited everybody to the party. In the same way God invites all of us into the kingdom of Heaven. If we refuse to accept his invitation we are like the guests who refused to come to the king's celebration.

Why was the man at the end of the story made to leave?

He had accepted the king's invitation, but he had not bothered to make the effort to dress for the occasion. If we accept God's invitation to join him in the kingdom of Heaven, then we must make the effort to do what is right and follow God's way or we cannot become part of the final celebration at the end of time.

Activity

Give each child a copy of an invitation to fill in and complete.

Closing Prayer

Lord Jesus,
you invite each one of us
to enter the kingdom of Heaven.
Help us to make the effort
to do things God's way,
so that we can accept your offer
and be ready to share in your glory
at the end of time.

INVITATION

Dear_ _ _ _ _ _ _ _

I invite you to follow me and to share in the celebration of God's glory at the end of time

Love from Jesus

REPLY

Dear_ _ _ _ _ _ _ _

Thankyou for inviting me to follow you so that I can share in the joy of your Kingdom

Love from_ _ _ _ _

Be ready

Reading

(cf Matthew 25:1-13)

One day Jesus told this parable, 'Ten bridesmaids were getting ready for a wedding, and together they went to greet the bridegroom, although they were not sure when he would come, or how long they would have to wait. Five of them were sensible girls who brought flasks of oil to refill their lamps; the other girls did not. The bridegroom was late, and after waiting all afternoon and all evening, the bridesmaids finally fell asleep. It was already midnight when somebody cried, "The bridegroom is coming! Quickly go and greet him!" The wise bridesmaids refilled their lamps and went to meet him, but the lamps of the foolish girls had gone out, and they had to go off to buy more oil. When they returned, the bridegroom and the five bridesmaids had already gone into the wedding hall.'

Discussion

Has anyone ever been a bridesmaid or a page at a wedding?

What did you wear and what did you do?

In the parable, who were the ten bridesmaids waiting for?

They were waiting to greet the bridegroom when he arrived, and to show him the way to the wedding hall. The bridegroom and bride are the ones who are getting married, becoming man and wife, so he is a very special person at the wedding.

Did they know when he would arrive?

They knew that he was coming, but they did not know the exact time he would arrive.

Why were the wise bridesmaids ready for his coming and the foolish bridesmaids not?

The five sensible girls knew that the bridegroom could arrive at any time – day or night! They brought flasks of oil for their lamps, in case the bridegroom was late, and their lamps had burned low. The foolish bridesmaids did not think ahead and brought no extra oil for their lamps. When the bridegroom suddenly arrived, they were not ready to meet him, and by the time they had filled their lamps, the bridegroom had already come and gone.

Jesus uses parables to give us a message. What do you think today's message is?

Jesus uses this story to tell us that we must always *be ready*. Like the bridesmaids, we know that Jesus will come again, but we do not know the exact day or time. The wise bridesmaids kept themselves ready so that they were not taken by surprise when the bridegroom finally arrived.

How can we keep ourselves ready for when Jesus returns?

If we can live each day as well as possible, and make each day our best, then we will always be ready to greet Jesus when he comes. By trying to be good and to live as Jesus taught us, ready to say sorry when we get things wrong and to forgive others, then we will be like the wise bridesmaids who kept their lamps burning, and be ready for Jesus when he comes.

Activity

Make the moving models of the lamp as shown. You may find it helpful to photocopy onto thin card.

Closing Prayer

Lord Jesus,
we know that one day you will return
and we will be with you in heaven.
Help us to make each day our best,
so that we will always be ready
to greet you.

'Be ready'
'Be ready'

Follow me

Reading

(cf Mark 1:14-20)

After John the Baptist had been arrested by Herod, Jesus began to preach to the crowds and proclaim the Good News. One day while walking beside the sea of Galilee he saw Simon Peter and his brother Andrew casting their nets to catch fish.

Jesus called out to them 'Come, follow me and I will make you fishers of people.' The brothers left their nets and followed him. Further along the shore Jesus saw James and his brother John who were mending nets with their father Zebedee. Jesus called them too, and at once they left their father and followed him.

Discussion

Can you remember the names of the brothers who left their boats and nets to follow Jesus?

Simon Peter and Andrew; James and John.

What did Jesus say to them?

He asked them to follow him and become 'fishers of people'. Jesus needed someone to help him with proclaiming the Good News of God, and to carry on his work when he had returned to his heavenly Father. These men would help him to lead people back to God, and to teach others of God's great love for them.

Many people followed Jesus and became his disciples, but Jesus chose a small number of them to carry on his work. How many did he choose, and can you remember some of their names?

Jesus chose twelve apostles. The name 'apostle' was given to a follower of Jesus who had been specially chosen. They were all close friends of Jesus, who were chosen to preach and perform miracles in his name.

The names of the twelve apostles were:

Simon Peter, Andrew, James, John, Philip, Bartholomew, Matthew, Thomas, (another) James, Thaddeus, Simon and Judas.

Does Jesus call us to follow him too?

Yes, Jesus calls us to follow him every day.

How can we do this?

To follow Jesus we do not usually have to leave home like the first disciples did! By loving God and our neighbours we can follow Jesus every day by living as Jesus taught us to.

Activity

The children can cut out these invitation cards. They can then fill in the blanks and decorate their cards.

Closing Prayer

Jesus, help us to follow you each day,
so that in our own small way
we can help to make our world a better place.

Dear ______

I invite you to follow me every day of your life

From Jesus

Dear Jesus

Thankyou for your invitation I would love to be one of your followers

From ______

THE KINGDOM OF GOD

READING

(cf Mark 4:30-34)

One day Jesus told this parable to the people: 'The kingdom of God is like a tiny mustard seed. Night and day, the little seed sprouts and grows. No-one sees it growing or knows how it happens. Until one day it has become a large and leafy shrub, and the birds of the air find shelter in its many branches.'

Jesus told the people many parables, and later when he was alone with his disciples he helped them to understand their messages.

DISCUSSION

Can you remember what a parable is?

A parable is a short, simple story which Jesus told to explain an important truth or teaching to the people.

In today's parable what did he talk about when explaining about the kingdom of God?

He talked about the tiny mustard seed, and the way that it grows into a large and sturdy plant, to explain how the kingdom of God can grow. The mustard seed plant and its seeds were a common sight in Israel.

Do you know any small seeds which grow into large plants or trees?

If possible have some familiar seeds displayed and discuss these with the children e.g. apple or orange pips, conkers, acorns, sunflower seeds. Show the children any pictures you can find of what mighty plants these small seeds can become.

Jesus often talked about the 'kingdom of God', and in today's parable he tries to explain more about this kingdom. What is the kingdom he talks about?

The kingdom of God is the new way of life that Jesus showed us. To live in this kingdom and be a part of it, means that we live as Jesus taught us. We put the love of God and our neighbours before anything else.

How is the kingdom of God like a mustard seed?

The kingdom of God grows from small beginnings like the tiny mustard seed. The word of God is planted in our hearts and, as we grow in kindness, love, understanding and forgiveness, we share it with others and in this way God's kingdom grows too.

ACTIVITY

Copy the illustration and ask each child to link each seed with the plant or tree which it becomes.

CLOSING PRAYER

Jesus taught us to pray, 'Thy kingdom come', and so we pray that the kingdom of God will grow in our daily lives as we say together:
Our Father . . .

Link each seed with the tree or plant it becomes

Messengers for Jesus

Reading

(cf Mark 6:7-13)

Jesus sent his twelve apostles out in pairs, to preach to the people and to cure the sick. He told them to take no money, no spare clothes and no food. 'If someone makes you welcome, then stay with them until your work is finished,' he said. 'But if people are unfriendly and do not want to listen to your message, then walk away and leave them to themselves.'

The apostles set off, and did everything as Jesus had said. Many people turned back to God after hearing their words, and others were cured in Jesus' name.

Discussion

If you were being sent off on a long journey, what sort of things would you want to pack?

- clothes to wear if the weather turned hot or cold
- food and something to drink
- several pairs of shoes
- toothbrush and toothpaste
- waterproof coat in case it rained
- money for bus or train fares

(Encourage the children to add their own ideas to the list.)

What did Jesus tell his apostles to take with them?

They were to go in the clothes they stood in, with nothing extra, except a stick in their hand to help them walk. They had no need of money or food, or any of the extra baggage we would want to take with us on a journey!

Why did Jesus want them to do this?

The most important thing the apostles carried was the message that Jesus had sent them with. This was the Good News that he had brought to share with the world, to lead people back to God's love and everlasting life; to love God and each other, to be forgiving and kind, and to live as Jesus had taught them. God would guide and look after the brave apostles on their mission, taking care of all their needs. Jesus knew that good people would welcome his apostles into their hearts and homes, and take care of them.

How do you think the apostles felt as they set off on their journeys?

They probably felt a mixture of excitement and fear. They did not know what sort of a welcome to expect from the people they preached to, or whether they would succeed in doing everything Jesus had asked them to do. They placed their trust in God to watch over and guide them.

How can we be like the apostles, and share the message of Jesus with the world around us?

We can share Christ's message with the people we meet every day, by making our thoughts, our words and our actions like those of Jesus. By living as he taught us to, and allowing the Holy Spirit to work through us, he can reach out and touch the lives of others, bringing them closer to God.

Activity

Using the cut-out picture help the children to provide the figure with everything he might need to help him on his journey through life to the kingdom of Heaven.

Closing Prayer

Lord Jesus, you chose the twelve apostles
to bring your message to the world.
You also chose to give each one of us life,
and to welcome us into the family of God.
Help us to share you message of love and truth
with the people we meet each day.

Love
GOODNESS
FORGIVENESS
JOY
Bread of life
Generosity
God's rules

The Shepherd and His Flock

Reading

(cf Mark 6:30-34)

After preaching to the people and curing many that were sick, the apostles returned to Jesus, and told him everything that they had said and done. As usual, crowds of people had followed them; the apostles were feeling tired and in need of a rest. Jesus said to them, 'We will go somewhere quiet and spend some time alone.'

However when Jesus and his friends arrived, a crowd of people had already gathered to meet them. When Jesus saw them, he was filled with pity, because they were like sheep without a shepherd to care for them. He sat down on the hillside and began to teach them.

Discussion

Where had the apostles been?

Jesus had sent them out to the villages to preach his message and heal the sick.

When they returned to Jesus, what did they find?

Wherever Jesus travelled, news soon reached the local people, and it was not long before a crowd of people flocked around him. The apostles were tired after their journeys and eager to spend time telling Jesus about everything that had happened. Jesus was surrounded by people wanting his attention.

What did Jesus suggest that they do?

Jesus suggested that they sail off to find some peace and quiet.

Things did not go quite as planned! What did they find when they moored their boat?

People had guessed their plan and when they arrived a crowd had already gathered.

What did Jesus do?

Did he grow impatient or angry?

Jesus felt a deep sense of love for his followers, and as always, put their needs before his own. The 'good shepherd' knew that these people were his flock. They relied on him to guide and look after them, just as a good shepherd guides and looks after his sheep. He would never let them down or turn them away.

Activity

Copy the adaptation of *Psalm 23* on to a large sheet of paper. Cut out a 'Good Shepherd' figure and enough sheep for each child. Use these to decorate the words of the prayer and encourage the children to illustrate the picture by drawing tufts of green grass, pools of water, a path etc. Alternatively hand out the colouring-in picture.

Closing Prayer

Read *Psalm 23* aloud together and discuss the words and illustrations with the children.

Psalm 23
The Good Shepherd takes care of all my needs:
He leads me to lush green meadows
and crystal clear pools.
He guides and protects me
and I grow strong in his care.
When night falls, I am not afraid,
for he is always beside me
to protect me from harm.
When he calls, I will follow,
knowing that his love for me
will last forever.

The good Shepherd takes care of all my needs. He leads me to lush green meadows and crystal clear pools. He guides and protects me and I grow strong in his care. When night falls, I am not afraid, for he is always beside me to protect me from harm. When he calls, I will follow, knowing that his love for me will last forever.

A CLEAN HEART

GOSPEL

(cf Mark 7:1-5, 14-15, 20-23)

One day the Pharisees noticed that Jesus and his disciples had not washed properly before eating. They asked Jesus, 'Why do you ignore the Jewish custom and eat your food with unclean hands?' Jesus answered, 'You have made the laws of men more important than the laws of God. You take great care to wash and keep your bodies clean on the outside. But you have forgotten that what is important is what lies inside – within your hearts. Ordinary dirt cannot make our hearts and lives unclean! Only words, thoughts and actions can do this. It is more important to God to have a good heart than clean hands.'

DISCUSSION

Why were the Pharisees angry with Jesus and his disciples?

They had disobeyed the custom of washing before a meal. Jewish laws expected people to wash their hands and faces before eating or praying.

Have you ever heard the saying, 'Cleanliness is next to Godliness'?

This sums up how the Pharisees felt about the importance of washing. It was very important to them to keep their bodies clean and free from stain, because they thought this brought them closer to God.

Why did Jesus not place such importance on these rules?

Jesus wanted to explain that dirt on the outside could not make a person unclean on the inside.

What do you think could make a person's heart unclean? (Encourage the children to make suggestions.)

When people have unkind thoughts, or act selfishly, or say something cruel, all these things make their hearts unclean. What goes on inside us is what really matters, and that is what matters most to God.

Another saying we often use is, 'You cannot judge a book by its cover.' Does this agree with what Jesus said?

A book may be old and grubby on the outside, but the story written inside could be the best story you've ever read. Just like books, the outward appearance of people can be misleading. We have to look into their hearts, and see what is inside, to know whether they are filled with God's goodness.

ACTIVITY

Dress the figure in the illustration in some simple cut-out clothes, with a jacket that opens at the front. Cut out a large heart shape, and help the children to write on it some of the things which make a person good inside. Stick this onto the figure, and make sure his jacket opens so that they can look inside.

CLOSING PRAYER

Father, pour your goodness into our hearts.
Help us to try not
to judge others by their appearance,
but to look for your goodness inside them.

A.
Fold
Fold
A. Glue to back of boy.
waistcoat opens to reveal heart.

JESUS IS THE SON OF GOD

READING

(cf Mark 8:27-35)

One day, while Jesus and his disciples were walking along, he asked them, 'Who do people say that I am?'

'Some say that you are John the Baptist, or Elijah or a prophet sent by God,' they answered.

Then Jesus asked them, 'Who do you think I am?'

It was Simon Peter who spoke up and said, 'You are Christ, the Son of God.'

After this, Jesus began to tell them how he would suffer and die, but would rise again after three days. Simon Peter argued with him, 'Lord we must not go to Jerusalem. These things must never happen!' Jesus said to him, 'Peter, we must do things God's way, even though it will not be easy.'

DISCUSSION

Why were people uncertain about who Jesus was?

Some people confused him with John the Baptist; some people had heard him preaching and thought that he was a prophet; to others he was simply the son of Joseph and Mary. Jesus appeared differently to different people.

Which apostle recognised who Jesus really was?

What did Simon Peter say?

'You are Christ, the Son of God.' The apostles had grown to know and love Jesus. On several occasions they had seen Jesus perform miracles which were only possible through the power of God.

If Jesus asked us the same question today, what would we say?

We know that Jesus is the Son of God, and saviour of the world. His love for us is unending and he is our best friend.

Why did Simon Peter get upset and argue with Jesus?

When Simon Peter heard that Jesus would suffer and die in Jerusalem, he wanted to save him and protect him from harm.

How did Jesus answer Simon Peter?

Jesus told him that it is more important to follow God's way than the way we might choose, even though sometimes this can mean having to put up with difficult times.

What does today's reading say to us?

We recognise Jesus as the Son of God. We are called to follow him like Simon Peter, but Jesus warns us that this will not always be easy. Just as he carried the cross for us before his death and resurrection, we will all have our own crosses or difficulties to bear in life. Our reward for this will be to share everlasting life with Jesus.

ACTIVITY

Give each child a cross shaped badge. Help them to pin these on after they have been coloured or decorated.

CLOSING PRAYER

We ask you, O Lord,
to help us through difficult times
when our troubles seem almost too much to bear.
Give us the strength to carry on
and to always do our best.
We ask this throught Christ our Lord.

THE CAMEL AND THE NEEDLE

READING

(cf Mark 10:17-25)

A man came to Jesus and asked, 'Master, what must I do if I want to share everlasting life with God?'

Jesus said, 'First, you must obey all of God's commandments.'

'I have always tried to live according to the rules of God,' the man said. Jesus looked at the man kindly, and saw his goodness and love. 'Then you must sell everything you own, and give all your money away. By doing this you will have riches in heaven, instead of here on earth.'

The man left Jesus sadly, because he was a very wealthy man. Jesus said to his friends, 'It is easier for a camel to pass through the eye of a needle, than for a rich man to enter the kingdom of heaven!'

DISCUSSION

What did the man want Jesus to tell him?

The man wanted to know what to do to make sure that he would go to heaven when he died.

What answer did Jesus give?

First, Jesus told the man that he must obey God's commandments. These rules were given to us by God, to help us choose between right and wrong. Then Jesus told the man that he must give away all his money and everything he owned.

How did the man feel when he heard the words of Jesus?

The man went away feeling sad, because although he was a good man, he did not want to give away all of his riches. Everything he owned meant more to him than the message of Jesus.

Jesus said that it was easier for a camel to pass through the eye of a needle than a rich man to enter the kingdom of Heaven.

Has anyone ever seen a camel?
How big are they?
How big is a needle?
What do we mean by the eye of the needle?

If you imagine how difficult it would be, for a large camel to climb through a needle, then you can understand what Jesus was trying to tell us!

(In this story Jesus was talking about a narrow gate leading into the city of Jerusalem, known as 'the Needle'. A camel could not pass through this gate easily, and in this way Jesus helped his followers to understand his message.)

Why did Jesus want the man to give up what he owned?

He wanted the man to understand that it is more important to have riches in heaven than riches on earth. Money can often make people greedy and selfish, and forgetful about the needs of others. God measures our wealth by our goodness, and whether we are generous and loving, and prepared to share what we have with others.

ACTIVITY

Photocopy the illustration. Give one of each to every child, and after colouring, help them to make a mobile.

CLOSING PRAYER

Lord, you see and remember
every act of kindness and generosity
and store up my treasure in heaven,
so that I can share everlasting life with you
at the end of time.

Gold

Master, let me see!

Reading

(cf Mark 10:46-52)

Jesus and his disciples were leaving Jericho with a crowd of followers, when they passed a blind beggar called Bartimaeus, sitting at the roadside. When he heard that Jesus of Nazareth had passed by, Bartimaeus began to shout loudly, 'Jesus have pity and help me!'

The crowd told him to calm down and be quiet, but Bartimaeus kept on shouting until Jesus heard his cries.

'Bring that man to me,' said Jesus, and they led Bartimaeus to him.

'What can I do for you?' he asked, and Bartimaeus said, 'Master, let me see!'

Then Jesus told him, 'Go. Because you believe in me your sight has returned.' Suddenly Bartimaeus could see clearly, and he set off at once to follow Jesus.

Discussion

Why was Bartimaeus begging at the roadside?

Because he could not see, Bartimaeus was unable to work to earn enough money to feed and clothe himself. He had to beg from passers by and rely on their kindness and generosity to save him from starvation.

What would you miss most if you could not see?

Encourage the children to share their thoughts.

What did Bartimaeus do when he heard that Jesus was close by?

He believed that Jesus could cure his blindness, and save him from a life of misery. He shouted loudly to attract Jesus' attention, and did not give up even when the crowd told him to be quiet.

What did Jesus do when he heard Bartimaeus cry for help?

Jesus did not let him down; and his cry for help was answered.

What did Bartimaeus do when he had been healed?

He followed Jesus, because his heart and mind, as well as his eyes, had been opened by God's love. Because of his faith, he could 'see' with his heart that Jesus was indeed the Son of God.

Activity

Assemble photocopies of the story into mini-books to be read aloud and coloured by the children.

Closing Prayer

Dear Jesus,
today we pray for blind people everywhere
and for those who help to care for them.
Thank you for the gift of sight,
allowing us to see the beauty of your world.

BARTIMAEUS
One day Jesus passed a blind beggar called Bartimaeus.
Bartimaeus shouted loudly–
Jesus have pity on me!
The crowd told him to be quiet, but Bartimaeus did not give up.
Jesus said–
Bring that man to me.
Jesus said–
Because you believed in me, you can see.
Bartimaeus shouted for joy and set off to follow Jesus.

Jesus is Born

Reading

(cf Luke 2:1-20)

Joseph and Mary arrived in Bethlehem to register for the census ordered by the Roman Emperor Augustus. The time came for Mary to have her baby, and he was born in a stable, because there was no room at the inn. She wrapped him in strips of cloth and laid him in a manger. On a hillside near the town, some shepherds were watching over their sheep. Suddenly, an angel appeared and the sky was filled with God's glory. The shepherds were terrified, but the angel said, 'Do not be afraid, for I have great news for you. Today a baby has been born in Bethlehem. He is Christ the Lord. You will find him lying in a manger.' The sky was filled with the sound of angels singing, 'Glory to God in the highest, and peace to all people on earth!' The shepherds hurried to Bethlehem and soon found the stable. There in the manger lay a tiny baby. They told Mary and Joseph what they had seen and heard that night, and they shared their amazement. Mary listened carefully and cherished all these things in her heart. The shepherds went back to their sheep on the hillside, singing God's praises, for everything had been as the angel had said.

Discussion

Use a prepared christingle as a visual aid for the discussion and ask the children if they know what the different parts of the christingle symbolise.

The christingle comprises:

1. An orange – this represents our world.
2. A candle pushed into the top – this represents the 'light' of the world.
3. A red ribbon around the orange – this represents the blood of Christ.
4. Four cocktail sticks with dried fruit stuck on – these represent the fruits of the earth, and the abundance of the four seasons.

The points to emphasise are:

1. That Jesus came to save the whole world and everyone in it.
2. His light reaches out to all people.
3. By dying on the cross, he shed his blood and saved us all from our sins.
4. God is generous and gave us all a wonderful world, with plenty of food and resources. We should not be greedy, and must always try to share what we can with others. This is very appropriate to remember at Christmas.

Activity

Help each child to make a christingle. Much of the preparation can be done in advance (they can be lit at home!) Afterwards sing carols with the children.

If plenty of notice is given, the children can bring non-perishable foodstuffs in to make up a hamper to be given to a worthy cause.

Closing Prayer

Dear Lord Jesus,
on this Christmas morning,
fill us with the joy and wonder
which the shepherds shared with Mary and Joseph.
May our hearts and our homes
be filled with the peace and love
you shared with the world.

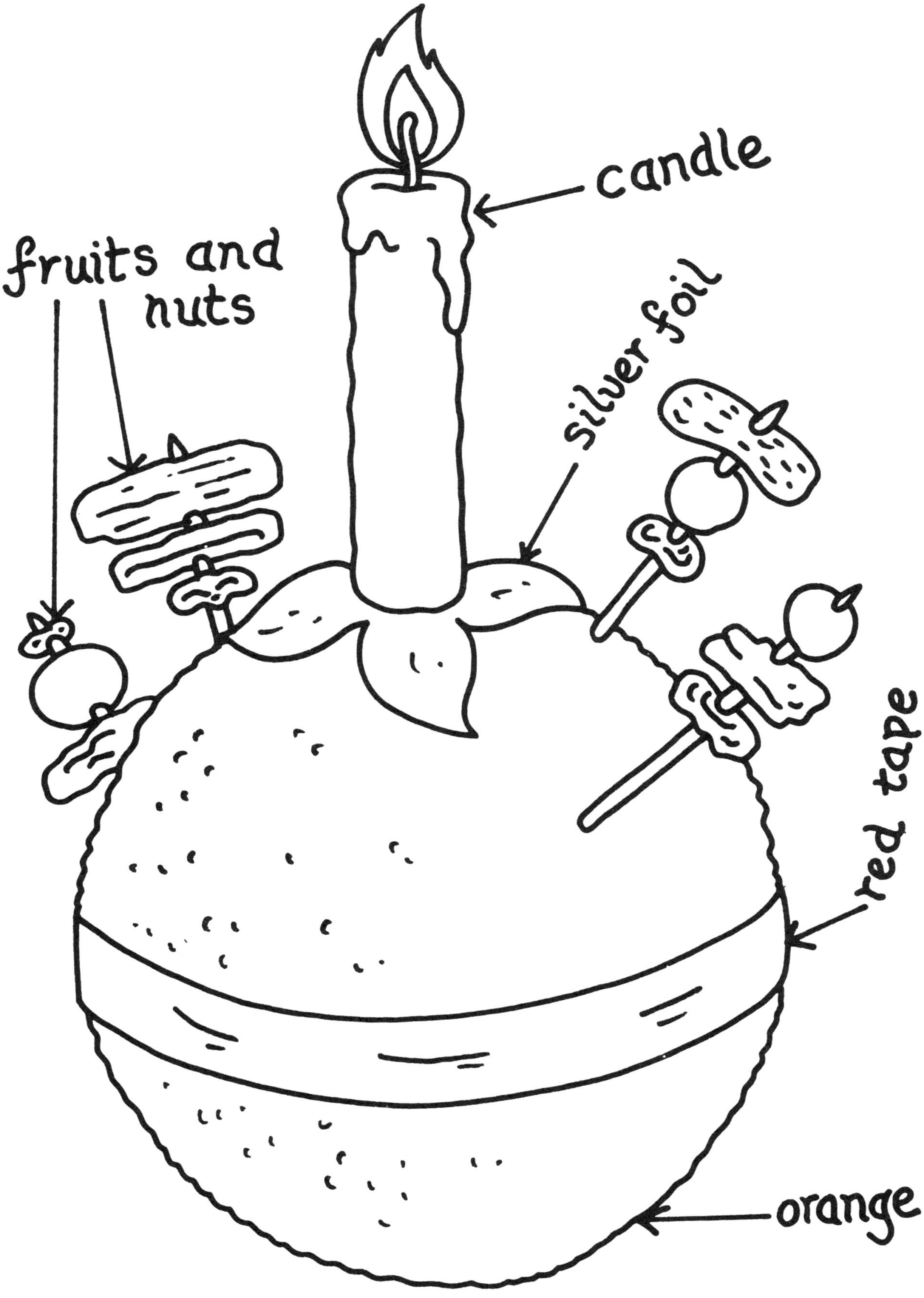
candle
fruits and nuts
silver foil
red tape
orange

Temptation in the Desert

Reading

(cf Luke 4:1-13)

Filled with the Holy Spirit, Jesus went into the desert to pray and be close to God.

He stayed there for forty days and during that time he had nothing to eat because he was fasting. He looked at the stones around him and knew that he could change them into bread; but he chose not to.

As he walked through the desert he knew that he could make himself king over all the land; but he chose not to.

When the forty days had passed Jesus went to the Temple in Jerusalem and climbed the stairs to the rooftop. He knew that if he jumped from the top, God would save him from harm, but he chose not to.

Discussion

How many days did Jesus spend in the desert?

Forty days is a long time! How many weeks are there in forty days?

There are almost six full weeks in forty days.

Jesus went into the desert to be close to God and to think. What do we call the time of year when we spend six weeks looking carefully at our lives and trying to grow closer to God?

Lent is the time when we stop and think about our lives, and turn back to God if we have wandered away from his love. During the six weeks of Lent we try to do something for God, to show how much we love him. It is a chance to say sorry for any mistakes we have made, and to make a fresh start.

Did Jesus find it easy in the desert?

On several occasions Jesus was tempted to take the easy way out, but he chose not to. During Lent we too will find it hard when we feel tempted to give up, but we must try not to.

Can you remember the three temptations which Jesus refused?

1. To turn the stones into bread. Jesus knew that God would provide him with everything he needed, and that he had been sent to take care of the needs of other people.
2. To become king of all the land. God is the king of all creation, and Jesus knew that His kingdom was more important than anything on earth.
3. To jump off the roof of the Temple and test God's love. Jesus trusted in his Father's great love; he did not need to ask God to prove it.

What can we learn from today's reading?

Jesus showed us the importance of spending some time looking at the good and bad things in our lives, and growing closer to God through prayer. Like us, he did not always find it easy to do, but with God's help he was able to choose to do the right thing, and to turn away from temptation. With help from our heavenly Father we can do the same!

Activity

Photocopy the illustration and help the children to complete the temptations which Jesus had to face.

Closing Prayer

Lord Jesus, you never gave up
even when you found it most difficult.
During the six weeks of Lent,
help us to be strong
and to keep our promises
as a sign of our love for you.

1. Turn the stones into
______
2. To become "
____ of all the land."
3. To ____ off the Temple walls and test
" God's love."

God's good news

Reading

(cf Luke 4:16-30)

Jesus began to read the words of the prophet Isaiah to the people in the synagogue at Nazareth. 'The spirit of God is with me and he has sent me to bring the Good News to the poor. I have come to bring freedom and to show people a new way.'

After Jesus had finished reading from the Scriptures he looked up at the crowd who were listening and said, 'Everything you have heard is coming true today, for I have been sent to bring the Good News to the world.'

The crowd grew angry when they heard this and said, 'Surely this is the son of Joseph the carpenter. He has no right to say such things!' Then they dragged him out of the Temple and away from the town, but Jesus slipped away before they could do him any harm.

Discussion

What did Jesus say to the people after he had finished reading from the Scriptures?

Jesus told the crowd that the words of the prophet Isaiah were coming true that very day. God's spirit was with him and he had come to share the message of God's love and mercy with all people.

Why did the crowd become angry?

Jesus was well known to many people in the crowd that day, because Nazareth was his home town where he had grown up. They all knew him as Mary and Joseph's son, an ordinary carpenter. They became angry when they heard him announce that he was the special one that the prophet Isaiah had foretold would come. They did not believe that there was anything special about this man.

What did they do to Jesus?

They dragged him from the synagogue and bustled him out of town.

How do you think Jesus felt?

Jesus knew that his own villagers and neighbours would find it hard to accept him as anything other than an ordinary carpenter. He probably felt sad and disappointed that they were not willing to listen and believe in his message.

Had Jesus been sent to bring the Good News to the Jewish people alone?

Jesus brought the message of God's love to be shared with *all* people, whatever their race or colour might be. God knows and loves each one of us, and we are all of equal importance to him. Jesus was always ready to welcome and love everyone, and we must be ready to do the same.

Activity

Photocopy the illustration to be coloured and pinned onto a display board.

Closing Prayer

Lord Jesus, open our ears to hear
the Good News of God's love
for each one of us.
Increase our faith and love for you,
we ask this through Christ our Lord.

JESUS THE CARPENTER.
THE SON OF GOD

Happiness is . . .

Reading

(cf Luke 6:17-23)

A large crowd of people had gathered to listen to Jesus who sat down and began to speak:

'Happy are the poor,
for their riches are stored in heaven.
Happy are the hungry,
because God will take care of their needs.
All who weep and are sad
will know only joy and laughter.
Be happy when people are cruel
or unkind because you follow me,
for your reward will be great in heaven.'

Discussion

Why had the crowd followed Jesus that day?

They wanted to listen to him teaching, and many had come hoping to be cured of their illnesses.

Jesus sat down and began to preach to them. Do you know what name is given to the sermon which he gave that day?

Today's reading is part of what is called 'The Sermon on the Mount' because Jesus spoke to the crowd as they gathered on a hillside or 'Mount' beside the Sea of Galilee.

St Luke tells us that Jesus gave four examples of true happiness. Can you remember what they were?

Help the children to recall the words,

1 Happy are the poor . . .
2 Happy are the hungry . . .
3 All who weep and are sad . . .
4 Be happy when people are cruel or unkind . . .

What was Jesus telling us in this sermon?

When we know that we are loved so much by God, that love brims over into our lives, we cannot help but share it with each other. It is through giving that we receive. So by sharing God's love which makes us so happy, with others, we make other people happy in turn, and our own happiness increases even more.

Worldly possessions and riches do not last forever, but God's love does and it is worth more than anything else. If we open our hearts and lives to God's love then we will know the true happiness that Jesus spoke of.

Activity

Photocopy and cut out a shape for each child. Ask them to draw themselves on the blank, and pin all the figures on a board with the caption 'Jesus makes us happy'.

Closing Prayer

Teach us, Lord,
that true happiness comes from you
and is worth more
than all our worldly possessions.

JESUS MAKES US HAPPY

GOOD FRUIT

READING

(cf Luke 6:43-45)

One day Jesus told this parable, 'Fruit that is rotten and bad can never grow on a strong and healthy tree, just as good fruit cannot grow on a tree that is sick and diseased.

'Different fruits grow on different trees, and everyone knows which fruit belongs to which type of tree. Like the tree and its fruit, the good will speak and act kindly, because of the goodness in their hearts.'

DISCUSSION

Does anyone have a fruit tree growing in their garden?

What type of tree is it?

What is the easiest way to tell the difference between an apple and a pear tree?

At certain times of the year, trees can be identified by the fruit growing on their branches. Apples only grow on apple trees, and pears only grow on pear trees!

(Show the children some pictures of different fruit trees and their fruit; a good gardening book should provide these.)

What do you need to get a good crop of tasty healthy apples?

An apple tree that is healthy and well cared for will usually produce lots of good fruit. A tree which is attacked by disease or pests, or whose branches and trunk become rotten, will produce only a few poor apples.

What is the message of today's parable?

Just as you can tell whether a tree is good or bad by the fruit it grows, so the words and actions of people reveal the state of their hearts. If we are healthy and strong, and full of God's goodness, then that goodness will show in our lives. If our hearts are selfish and unkind, then we will be selfish and unkind to people.

How can we make sure our lives are filled with God's love and goodness?

God comes to each one of us in a very special way when we receive the Holy Spirit. Just as a tree needs to be nourished to produce good fruit, so we need the Holy Spirit to nourish us. We invite Jesus into our lives and the goodness he shares with us overflows into our daily words and actions.

ACTIVITY

The children can cut out the good apples and stick them in the tree. Help them to assemble the pictures on a background after they have been coloured, and add the caption: 'The Fruits of Goodness'.

CLOSING PRAYER

Lord Jesus,
may people see the fuits of your love
and goodness in our words
and the way we treat other people.

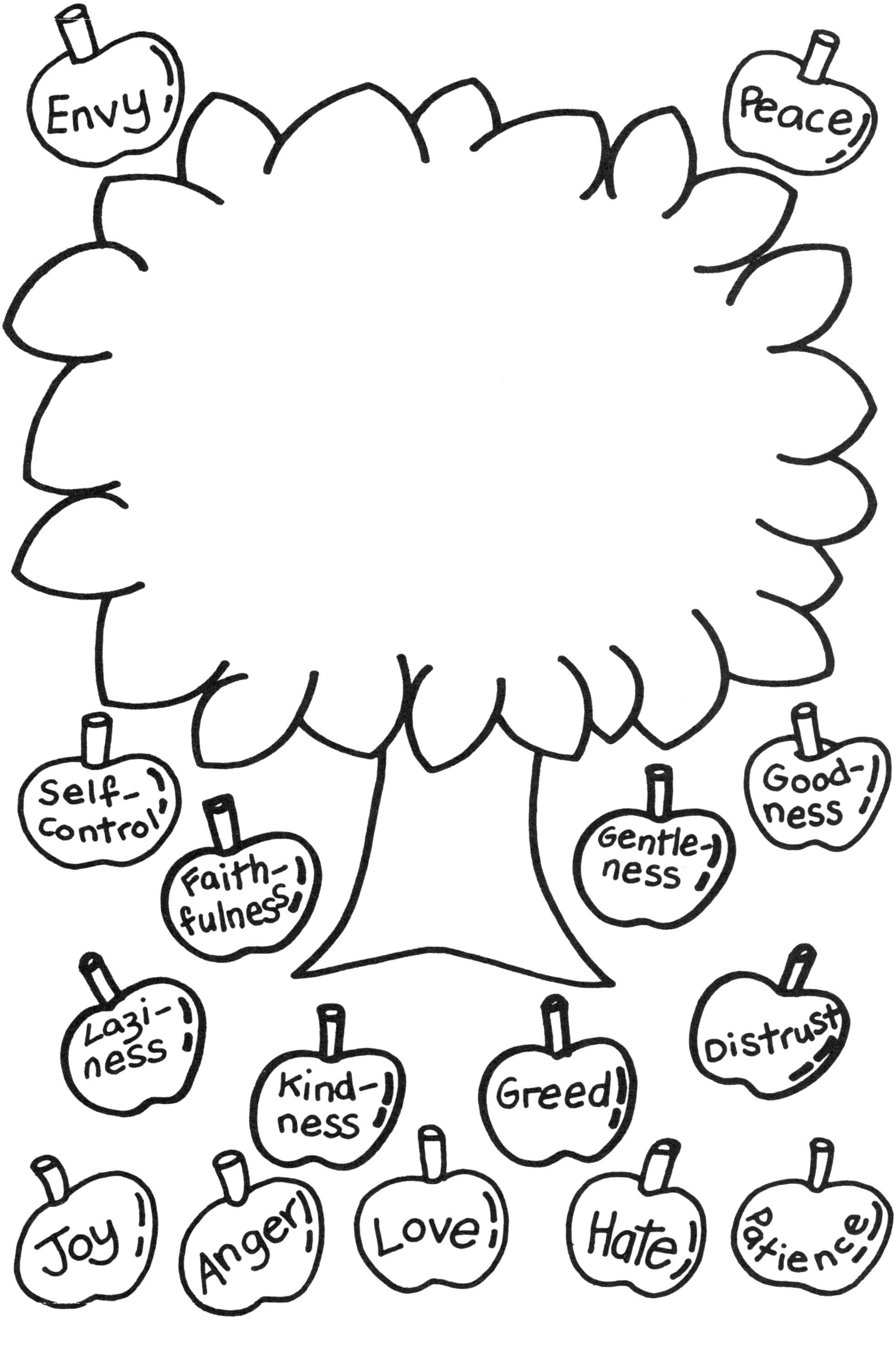
Envy
Peace
Self-control
Faith-fulness
Gentle-ness
Good-ness
Lazi-ness
Kind-ness
Greed
Distrust
Joy
Anger
Love
Hate
Patience

THE GOOD SAMARITAN

READING

(cf Luke 10:29-37)

A man once said to Jesus, 'I know that I should love God with all my heart, and love my neighbour too. But who is my neighbour?'

Then Jesus told him this story, 'One day a man was travelling from Jericho to Jerusalem, when a gang of robbers attacked him. They beat him up, and after stealing everything he had, they left him lying injured by the roadside. A short time later one of the temple priests passed that way, but he crossed the road and walked on by. Soon, another traveller came, but he too passed on by. Then a Samaritan happened to pass, and when he saw the injured man he took pity on him. He bandaged his wounds, and carried him on horseback to a nearby inn. There he cared for him and when the time came to leave, he left the innkeeper enough money to pay for the man's room until he was better.' Jesus then asked the man, 'Which man in the story was a good neighbour?'

'The one who helped the wounded traveller', he answered. 'Go then and do the same for anyone who needs your help,' said Jesus.

DISCUSSION

This story is often called the 'good Samaritan'.

What was a Samaritan?

A Samaritan was someone who came from a region of Palestine called Samaria. The Samaritans and the Jews had been enemies since Old Testament times. The good Samaritan did not worry about the injured man's religion or race, instead he saw someone who needed his help, and was filled with a sense of love and pity. Even today when someone does a good deed for another person, we often call them a 'good Samaritan'.

What did the other men do when they saw the injured traveller?

They crossed the road and walked on by. They were not prepared to put themselves to any trouble, and ignored the needs of the man lying on the roadside. Today, too many people are in a hurry, and are unwilling to stop and offer help to someone who needs it.

(Perhaps you or the children have had such an experience?)

From the story which Jesus told, who is our neighbour?

Our neighbour is whoever we meet, whatever their race, religion or colour might be. When a fellow human being is suffering, or needs our help, then we should show the same loving concern and compassion as the good Samaritan.

Jesus told the man to go away and be a good Samaritan. How can we do the same?

By treating everyone with kindness and love, whether it is at school, at home or when playing with friends. By loving one another as we love ourselves we will please our heavenly Father.

ACTIVITY

Either photocopy the story of the good Samaritan for each child, or copy each picture onto a separate sheet of paper to be coloured and displayed.

CLOSING PRAYER

Lord,
today we pray for anyone
who needs a good Samaritan;
give each of us the courage
to stop and help
when our neighbour needs us

THE GOOD SAMARITAN
A man was returning from Jericho to Jerusalem.
A gang of thieves attacked and robbed him.
No one would stop to help.
Everyone walked on by.
A good Samaritan took care of the traveller.
Jesus said, "Help whoever needs you."

The rich man

Reading

(cf Luke 12:16-21)

One day Jesus told this parable, 'Once there was a rich man who owned many farms. One year the harvest was so good that the man could not store all of it in his many barns. "I will build bigger and better barns," he said, "and then I will be so rich that I will have nothing to worry about."

'But God said to the man, "You are a foolish man! When you die, what use will your worldly riches be, because in the eyes of God you are poor indeed."'

Discussion

Why did the rich man need to build bigger and better barns?

That year there was a bumper harvest and he could not fit all the crops into his barns to be stored.

If he had been a kind and generous man, what could he have done with the extra food he had?

The man was already rich, and did not really need to worry about storing the extra harvest. Instead of being selfish and greedy he could have stored up his treasure in heaven by giving some of the food to people who needed it more than he did.

What kind of treasure did the rich man store up for himself?

He busied himself making money, and thought that if he had enough then he would be a truly happy man.

What sort of riches should the man have stored up for himself?

Money and possessions do not make us rich in the eyes of God. By living as Jesus taught us and sharing in God's kingdom now, we will store up our treasure in heaven. Every good deed and word of kindness is more precious to God than money can ever be. When we die, whatever money or possessions we have are left behind us, but our goodness will last forever and bring us everlasting happiness.

Activity

Give each child a copy of the maze and ask them to show the rich man the way to heaven.

Closing Prayer

(cf Psalm 119:36-37)

Lord, help me
to store up my riches in heaven
and not just on earth,
and to know what is truly important
so that I do not waste my time
on worthless things.

LOVE
Kindness
BEING generous
TREASURE IN HEAVEN
Sharing
Finish
Lead the Rich man to the real Treasure!
Start

JESUS TRUSTS US

READING

(cf Luke 12:41-48)

One day Jesus told this story, 'A man gave orders to his two servants, and trusted them to be carried out while he was away. One servant did what his master had told him, even though he did not know when his master would return. The other servant betrayed his master's trust and did not carry out his wishes.

When the master returned unexpectedly, the good and trustworthy servant was generously rewarded, but the other servant was punished and sent away.'

DISCUSSION

What did the master expect his servants to do?

The master trusted his servants to carry out his orders while he was away.

Did the servants deserve their master's trust?

One of the servants did what his master asked. The other servant was lazy, and without his master to watch him, he avoided the work he had been given to do. The first servant deserved his master's trust but the second servant did not.

Before Jesus returned to his Father in Heaven, what work did he trust his disciples to do when he had gone?

Jesus said *(cf John 15:14-16, 27)*, 'You are my friends if you do what I command. I chose you to go out and bear fruit which will last forever. You will be my witnesses because you have been with me from the beginning.'

Jesus trusted his disciples to carry on his work when he had gone: curing the sick, forgiving sinners, performing miracles in his name, sharing the teachings of Christ with the world and the Good News of God's love for all people.

Did the disciples deserve Jesus' trust?
Did they do what he had asked?

After the Holy Spirit came to the disciples at Pentecost, they went out and began to teach the Gospel to the world. They did what Jesus had asked them to do, and shared with others everything they had seen and heard.

Who is trusted to do the work of Jesus today?

Each one of us, in our own way, has a part to play in sharing the Good News of the Gospel with other people. As Christians we are followers, or disciples, of Christ. Just as the first disciples were trusted, so Jesus trusts each one of us to carry on his work.

How can we do this in our everyday lives?

In our own way we can share Christ's message with others, by our words and actions and by being kind, forgiving and loving, just as Jesus was.

If we have been trustworthy what will happen at the end of time when Jesus returns?

We will be generously rewarded for our loyalty and goodness by sharing in the joy and happiness of everlasting life in heaven.

ACTIVITY

Photocopy the activity sheet and if necessary help the children to fill in the blanks.

CLOSING PRAYER

Lord Jesus,
send your Holy Spirit to each one of us
so that we can carry on the work
with which you trust us.

Write down the first letter of each object to find out what Jesus trusts us to do.

___ ___ ___ ___ ___

___ ___ ___   ___ ___ ___ ___

___ ___ ___ ___   ___ ___

___ ___ ___ ___

___ ___ ___ ___

Few will be chosen

Reading

(cf Luke 13:22-30)

On the way to Jerusalem, someone stopped Jesus and asked, 'Master, will many be saved at the end of time?'

Jesus answered, 'Many will try to enter the kingdom of God but few will succeed; some will leave it too late and find they have missed their chance of everlasting happiness. So take care and be ready! At the end of time, people will be called from far and wide to rejoice in God's heavenly kingdom.'

Discussion

Why will many try to enter the kingdom of God but not succeed?

Jesus showed us the way to God's kingdom by his actions and words. If we live in God's way then we will share everlasting happiness with him at the end of time. This is not easy to do, and throughout our lives we will often fail and make mistakes. With God's help we can carry on, but many will turn away or give up altogether.

Why will some people leave it too late to claim their place in heaven?

No one knows when Jesus will return, and he told many parables to explain that we must always be ready for this moment (e.g. the parable of the watchful servants, *Luke 12:35-40;* the parable of the wise bridesmaids, *Matthew 25:1-13.*) We must make each day of our life pleasing to God, instead of promising to be good tomorrow, or next week, or sometime after. If we do not try *now*, then we might miss our chance of happiness.

Can anyone belong to the kingdom of God?

Jesus taught us that God is 'our Father' and that we are all brothers and sisters in the one family of God. At the end of time, God will gather his children from all the nations, whatever their colour or language, to take their place in his Kingdom.

What must each of us try to do today and every day?

To follow Jesus day by day and trust in him to help us do what is right. One good way to begin doing this is to say a 'morning offering', when we offer all our thoughts and actions of the coming day to God.

Activity

Photocopy the morning offering prayer to be read aloud together before being coloured.

Closing Prayer

Lord Jesus,
help us to live in God's way
and always be ready to greet you.
Though we make many mistakes,
grant us your forgiveness
and pour your grace into our hearts
to make us strong again.

MORNING OFFERING

Father in Heaven
I give you today,
all that I think,
and do, and say.
I give you the good times
as well as the bad,
the times when I'm happy,
the times when I'm sad.
Fill me with grace
and make me strong.
With you at my side
I won't go wrong.

Amen.

THE FIRST WILL BE LAST

READING

(cf Luke 14:1, 7-14)

One day Jesus went to the house of a Pharisee to share a sabbath meal. Many guests had been invited and, noticing how they rushed to take the best seats, Jesus said to them: 'When you are invited for a meal, do not take the best place because a more important guest might be there. You will be embarrassed when the host asks you to move and give up your seat. Instead, always sit in the least important place, so that when you are moved to a better seat others will see how much you are respected.'

Then Jesus said, 'Do not invite people to eat with you because you know they can invite you back. Be generous and invite those who cannot repay your kindness. You will be rewarded for your goodness at the end of time.'

DISCUSSION

Have you ever rushed to get the 'best seat' before someone else?

- perhaps to get a particular seat on the school bus
- to get a seat with the best view at a film or show
- to sit closest to the food at a party

All of us have done this at one time or another! Jesus wanted us to realise that when we do such a thing, we put ourselves before others, thinking that we are more important than other people.

What did Jesus tell us to do instead?

We should try to put others first and act without selfishness or pride. God is not impressed by greatness or rank, but by someone who acts humbly and shows kindness towards other people.

In what other way did Jesus suggest that we could be considerate?

Jesus used the example of inviting someone for a meal without expecting to be invited back. Often we do a 'good turn' for someone but expect them to repay our kindness in some way. Jesus taught us that if we act with unselfish kindness in this life, then God will repay our goodness in the next.

How can we put the words of Jesus into practice?

Instead of pushing to the front or grabbing the best seat, think of others first, and act thoughtfully instead of selfishly. Don't invite someone to play just so that they can invite you back; or share a toy because you expect one in return.

ACTIVITY

Jesus calls us to be less selfish and more loving. Colour the pictures which put others first, and cross out the pictures which show selfish and thoughtless actions.

CLOSING PRAYER

Jesus,
help me to put others first,
and to be generous and kind
without counting the cost.

Doing the washing-up for Mum.
Avoiding the washing-up.
Watching their favourite programme.
Watching my favourite programme.
Stopping someone joining my game.
Asking someone to join my game.

THE SON WHO CAME BACK

READING

(cf Luke 15:11-24)

One day Jesus told this story, 'There was a man who had two sons and the younger one came to his father and said, "Father, give me everything that will one day belong to me, so I can enjoy my riches now."

'The father did this, and the younger son set off to look for adventure. He travelled to a distant land and spent all his money enjoying himself.

'There was a famine in that land, and the young man found himself penniless and hungry. "If I stay here I will surely starve," he thought, so he decided to return to his father and ask for his forgiveness. The father saw his son coming and ran to welcome him. As he hugged him, the young man said, "Father I am *so* sorry. I no longer deserve to be called your son." But his father told his servants to prepare a feast and to bring the finest clothes, and they began to celebrate.'

DISCUSSION

Why did the son decide to leave home?

He wanted to enjoy himself and to see the world while he was young.

How do you think his father felt?

His father was probably very sad. He loved his son and wanted to make him happy, so he was ready to give him what he asked for and to watch him leave.

Do you think the son was selfish?

The young man thought only of his own needs and happiness. He did not worry about the unhappiness he would cause.

Why did the young man decide to return home?

When he was starving, he realised that he would always be welcomed and cared for at home. When we are having a bad time, we know that we can turn to our families at home for help and support because they love and care for us.

The father saw his son coming in the distance and ran to greet him. What does this tell us about him?

The father was looking out for his son and hoping that one day he would return. He never stopped loving him and ran to welcome him and show how pleased he was to have him home again.

What did the son say to his father?

The son asked his father to forgive him for being foolish and selfish. The father forgave him at once and celebrated his return.

Why did Jesus tell this story?

Jesus wanted us to understand that whatever we do wrong, we can always come back to our heavenly Father to ask for his forgiveness and know that He will welcome us with open arms. God feels sad and waits patiently for our return when we turn away from Him.

ACTIVITY

Photocopy the pictures telling the story of 'The son who came back' and help the children to make and colour their mini books.

CLOSING PRAYER

Lord, you gave your love and peace to us.
Help us to make our world a happier place
by sharing that love and peace
with each other.

THE SON WHO CAME BACK
Father, give me what belongs to me.
The son left and his father was very sad.
He spent all his money enjoying himself.
I will go to my father and say sorry.
His father saw him coming and ran to greet him.
There was great celebration because the son had come back to his father.

Always be honest

Reading

(cf Luke 16:10-11)

Jesus said, 'When a person is honest about the small things in life, then they will be honest about more important things too. If you cannot be trusted with something as unimportant as money, how can you be trusted with the most precious treasure of all?'

Discussion

If you saw someone dropping a pound coin without noticing, what would you do?

You would have to choose between being honest, and giving the coin back, or dishonest, and keeping the coin yourself. When a person is filled with the spirit of God's goodness, they can be trusted to make the right choice. A good person will always be honest, however great or small the amount of money may be.

Listen to this short story:

Peter had been saving his pocket money for a long time and just needed one more pound to afford the football he wanted so much. One day while shopping with his mum, he noticed that an old lady had dropped some money as she struggled to put it in her purse. The coin rolled across the floor and lay unnoticed. Peter picked it up and found to his delight that it was a pound, just what he needed! (At this point ask the children what they think Peter should do, before reading on to see if they were right!)

. . . Peter took the coin over to the old woman who thanked him for his kindness and honesty. Peter smiled, feeling very good inside.

Why do you think Peter felt good inside? – Peter had chosen God's way, by being honest and truthful. His actions had made the old woman very happy, and seeing her happiness made him feel good inside. We all know how wonderful we feel when we show someone that we care about them. Peter felt the joy of sharing God's love and knowing that God was pleased with him.

What is the most precious treasure of all which Jesus trusts us with?

The most precious treasure of all is the love of our heavenly Father which means more than all our worldly possessions. Money cannot make us happy, because true happiness comes from loving God. We are free to live as we choose, because God trusts us to do what we know is right.

Activity

Either use the activity sheets or help each child to fold a sheet of paper in half to find the middle. On one half, ask them to draw a picture of themselves in the playground, with a £1 coin they have found at their feet. Give each child a 'choice wheel' and a butterfly pin and help them to pin it on the other half of the paper. Get the children to draw an arrow and, turning the wheel, to point to whatever choice they think they should make. Discuss!

Closing Prayer

Lord, help us to be truthful and honest with each other and to be guided by your goodness.

"Be Honest"

Turn
Tell no-one
Put it in my pocket
Take it to my teacher
Buy some sweets
Turn

Lazarus and the Rich Man

Reading

(cf Luke 16:19-26)

One day Jesus told this story, 'Once there was a rich man who had fine clothes, and the best of everything that money could buy. He spent his time enjoying himself and feasting with his rich friends.

'On the street outside his house lay a poor man called Lazarus who was thin and hungry, and covered in sores. Lazarus would gladly have eaten the rich man's scraps, if they had been offered to him.

'Lazarus died and went to heaven where he was truly happy at last. When the rich man died he went to hell, and seeing Lazarus so happy, he cried out to him for help. But God asked the rich man, "Did you help when Lazarus cried out for food? Did you care for him when he was ill and had nowhere to go? You thought only of yourself, and gave up the chance of everlasting happiness with me."'

Discussion

How did the rich man spend his time and his money?

All his time was spent on himself and doing the things which made him happy.

Who lay unnoticed outside the rich man's house?

Lazarus had no home and no money. He sat outside the rich man's house, and begged for food.

Have you ever seen anyone begging?

Many poor people beg for money to buy food and clothes. Often they are homeless and have nowhere to sleep, and we want to help them but don't quite know how. There are many homes and hostels where donations of food, clothes and even toys are gratefully received. Each of us in our own way, however small, should help wherever we can.

What did the rich man do about Lazarus?

The rich man did absolutely *nothing!* He was so concerned about his own happiness that he did not even notice Lazarus lying outside his house.

What do you think the rich man should have done?

(Encourage the children to share their ideas.)

In this story Jesus wanted to show us that being well off and comfortable often makes us 'blind' to the needs of people around us. We can become selfish and self-centred, caring only about our own happiness. We should not forget that our words and actions in life will decide whether we share God's everlasting happiness or, like the rich man, pay for our greed and selfishness.

Activity

Copy and cut out the two figures, the house, path and some palm trees. After colouring these separately stick them onto a large sheet of paper and encourage the children to fill in the background.

Closing Prayer

Father in Heaven,
bless all the homeless people in our world,
and those who have to beg for their food.
Open our eyes to their needs
so that we can help them in whatever way we can.

Don't give up

Reading

(cf Luke 18:1-8)

Jesus told this story: In a certain town there was a judge who was often unjust and unfair. A woman in the town asked the judge to help her settle a quarrel with her neighbour. The judge was not interested in the woman's problem and sent her away. The woman did not give up! She came back every day, day in and day out, until the judge could not stand being pestered any more. 'I must give this woman what she wants,' he said, 'or she will never give me any peace.'

Then Jesus said, 'If such a man can finally listen and do what is asked of him, how much more will my heavenly Father do for you if you keep on asking.'

Discussion

Why did the woman keep on pestering the judge?

She was determined that the judge would hear her request, listen carefully to what she wanted and then respond.

Did the woman's persistence pay off?

No-one likes to feel pestered or nagged and after a while the judge finally agreed to what the woman wanted.

Have you ever pestered anyone for something you really wanted?

What happened?

Encourage the children to reflect on their own experiences.

What was Jesus trying to tell us in this parable?

That if we ask God for something he will hear our prayers and answer them. Because we do not understand God or his plans for us, sometimes we feel disappointed when he doesn't seem to give us what we want or need, but we must not give up or stop asking, instead we must learn to put our trust in God because he will always do what is best for us.

Activity

Photocopy the activity sheet and see if the children can discover the woman's message to them!

Closing Prayer

Let us say together the prayer which Jesus himself taught us: Our Father . . .

Believe in me

Reading

(cf Luke 21:5-7, 12-19)

Jesus was at the Temple in Jerusalem when he overheard some of the crowd talking.

'This Temple was built to last forever!' they said.

But Jesus told them, 'One day, everything, including this Temple will be destroyed.'

'When will this happen?' they asked him.

'Do not be afraid,' said Jesus, 'the time for all this to happen is still a long way off. Before then many will suffer because they are my followers. I will give them courage and strength, and they will be rewarded for their faith and goodness by my heavenly Father.'

Discussion

What did Jesus mean when he said that one day everything, including the Temple would be destroyed?

Jesus was talking about the end of the world, when he will return in power and glory. Buildings and possessions will not last forever, but love and goodness can never be destroyed.

Did Jesus tell the people when this would happen?

Jesus did not tell them an exact day or time, but that the end of the world would not come until many people had suffered because they believed in him.

Why is being a Christian not always easy?

As Christians we believe in Jesus and everything he taught us. We share one faith which is a gift from God. Jesus expects us to share that faith with others, through our words and by the lives we lead. Many of the early Christians suffered and died for their faith, because others would not believe in Jesus. Today it is not always easy to follow Christ's way of love, and to build our lives around his teachings, but Jesus promised to give us the strength and courage that we need.

How will Christians be rewarded for their faith?

If we choose to follow Jesus and to live as he taught us, then we will be rewarded for our goodness by sharing everlasting happiness with God at the end of time.

Activity

Cut an oval shape from card for each child, and punch two holes opposite each other at the ends of the oval. Write 'Believe in' on the top half of one side above the holes. Turn the oval over so that the words are upside down and face down. Write 'Jesus' above the holes as before. Loop elastic bands or pieces of wool through the holes. After colouring in the letters and decorating the ovals, the children can wind the ovals to twist the bands. Then pull apart and see the message they have written.

Closing Prayer

Heavenly Father,
thank you for the gift of faith
which each of us has been given.
Help us to share it
with whoever we meet.

WE BELIEVE

IN JESUS

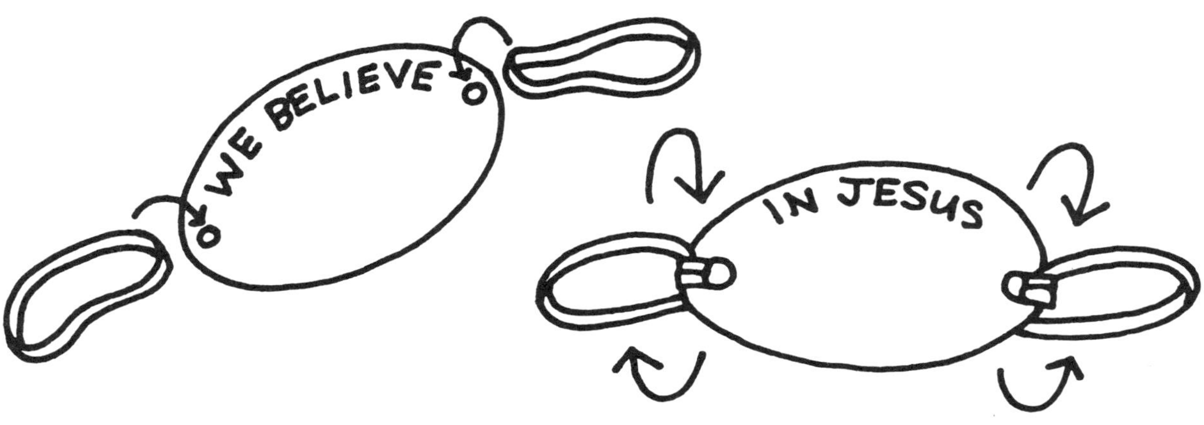
WE BELIEVE
IN JESUS

The road to Emmaus

Reading

(cf Luke 24:13-35)

Early one morning two disciples of Jesus were walking sadly towards a village called Emmaus. They felt totally miserable as they talked about the events of the past few days, and the death of Jesus. As they walked, Jesus himself joined them, but they did not recognise him. Jesus asked them, 'What are you talking about together?' One of them answered, 'Surely you must have heard about what happened to Jesus of Nazareth! He was handed over to the chief priests and the Roman Governor who had him crucified. We believed that he was the Saviour sent by God. We have heard that his body is missing from the tomb where they laid him, but we do not know what has happened.'

Jesus said to them, 'Do you not believe what the prophets have foretold?' and he began to explain to them the prophecies about himself in the Old Testament. When they arrived at Emmaus, the disciples asked Jesus to stay and share a meal with them. When they were at supper Jesus took some bread, blessed it, broke it and gave it to them. At that moment they saw clearly that the stranger was in fact Jesus, but he had already disappeared from their sight. 'Of course it was the Lord,' they said, 'Remember how our hearts seemed to burn as he shared the Scriptures with us. How could we have been so blind!' At once, they returned to Jerusalem to tell the other disciples that Jesus had risen from the dead, and that they had known him in the breaking of the bread.

Discussion

Have you ever felt really disappointed when something has gone wrong?

- you have planned a picnic but at the last moment it rains
- a friend is coming to play but has to cancel because they are ill
- your football team almost makes it to the top of the league and then loses all its important matches

You can imagine then how the disciples of Jesus felt! They were terribly disappointed and depressed about his death. Everything had gone so wrong during the past few days.

How could this have happened when they had seen Jesus working so many miracles?

At first, did they believe that Jesus had risen from the dead?

They knew that his body was missing from the tomb, and they did not understand the things that Jesus had said about 'rising from the dead'. They were quite sure that people did not come back to life.

What made them realise who he was?

He blessed the bread and broke it. It was his special way of sharing a meal with his friends. Through sharing God's word and the breaking of bread, their eyes were 'opened' and they could 'see' clearly.

Activity

Either give each child a copy of the illustration to colour, or make a larger picture, and after colouring add cut-out loaves etc. to the scene.

Closing Prayer

Lord Jesus,
each time we come together
to share in the breaking of bread,
help us to recognise you
and to feel our hearts burn with your love.

JESUS BLESSED THE BREAD
AND BROKE IT.

Christ's witnesses

Reading

(cf Luke 24:36-48)

The disciples who had met Jesus on the road to Emmaus were telling the others what had happened, when suddenly Jesus appeared amongst them. At first they were terrified, because they thought that they had seen a ghost! Then Jesus said to them, 'Peace be with you,' and seeing that they were still scared, he added, 'Do not be afraid. Why do you doubt what you can see? Please, look at my wounds and see that I am not a ghost. Touch me. A ghost has no flesh or bones as I have!' They were overjoyed but still filled with disbelief. Then Jesus asked them for something to eat and they watched as he ate some grilled fish.

Then he began to explain the Scriptures to them, so that finally, they understood what scripture had said about the Messiah suffering and rising after three days. Jesus said to them 'You are my witnesses because you have seen all these things happen.'

Discussion

How would you feel if you saw a ghost?

How did Jesus calm and reassure his terrified disciples?

He appeared, saying the words, 'Peace be with you,' and told them not to be afraid. Then he showed them his wounds to convince them that he really had risen from the dead.

Even after showing the disciples his wounds did they really believe what they were seeing?

Although they were overjoyed to see Jesus again, they were totally dumbfounded to find that he was really alive, so Jesus ate a piece of fish to convince them that he was real and not a ghost!

Jesus told the disciples that they were his witnesses. What did he mean?

The disciples had seen and heard for themselves all the marvellous things that Jesus had done. He would send them out to give evidence or proof of this by the way they lived, the miracles they would perform in his name, and the things they would teach.

Can we be witnesses for Christ?

Jesus said, 'Blessed are those who have not seen and yet *believe.*' We may not have seen all these things with our own eyes but we believe. Each of us can be a witness for Christ by living God's way, as Jesus showed us. When we become members of the Christian family we are called to follow Christ and be a witness for him every day of our lives.

Activity

On a large sheet of paper draw a representative map of the world (it does not need to be accurate!) or if available, use a large map of the world. Photocopy the various modes of transport that the apostles might have used. After colouring, help the children to add them to the map, with large red arrows pointing in various directions. Add the caption, 'Witnesses to the world'.

Closing Prayer

Lord Jesus,
send us your Spirit
to give us the strength
to live as you taught us.
Help us to bear witness to you
by our actions and our words.

Lamb of God

Reading

(cf John 1:35-39)

John the Baptist was standing with two of his followers when he saw Jesus walking by. 'There is the Lamb of God,' he said, looking at Jesus. On hearing this, the two men left John and followed Jesus. Seeing that they were following him, Jesus turned and asked, 'What do you want with me?' 'We would like to know where you live,' they answered. 'Come with me and see,' Jesus said. So they followed him to his house and stayed with him for the rest of the day.

Discussion

How did John the Baptist describe Jesus?

As the 'Lamb of God'.

Why did John compare Jesus to a lamb?

To encourage discussion, try to provide a picture of a lamb for the children to look at.

Lambs are meek and gentle, just as Jesus was. Often they were offered by people as a sacrifice to God to show their love for him. Jesus was sent by his heavenly Father to proclaim the Good News and to save us. Like a lamb, he was prepared to be sacrificed, to suffer and to die out of love for us, so that we could share everlasting life in heaven.

When John pointed Jesus out, what did the two men do?

John had often told his followers about the one who was to come after him: the Messiah promised by God. John urged his followers to go with Jesus and to become his disciples, so they followed him.

What did Jesus do when he saw the two men following him?

He invited them to join him and took them to his home. They were completely amazed by this meeting, and marvelled at everything Jesus said.

One of these men became an apostle of Jesus. Do you know his name?

His name was Andrew and he was the brother of Simon Peter. After this first meeting with Jesus he ran to tell his brother Simon Peter all about Jesus because he believed that Jesus really was the Saviour of the World.

Activity

Give each child a cut-out sheep and a square of coloured paper with the caption 'Jesus is the Lamb of God' written on it. Ask them to glue the sheep onto the piece of card and then stick on some cotton wool as its fleece. Attach a piece of thread to each card and suspend these from a mobile display.

Closing Prayer

Andrew saw the Lamb of God and followed him.
Help us to follow you every day, Lord,
so that others will know that we are Christians
and will follow you too.

Jesus is the lamb of God

THE GOOD SHEPHERD

READING

(cf John 10:11-15)

One day Jesus said, 'I am the Good Shepherd, who is ready to die for his sheep. A man who is hired to look after the flock does not really care about it because he knows that the sheep do not really belong to him. When the hungry wolf appears, the man runs away, and the sheep are scattered. I know each of my sheep by name, and they know the sound of my voice. They will always follow me and I am ready to give up my life for them.'

DISCUSSION .

What is a shepherd?

What do you think makes a good shepherd?

A good shepherd cares for all the needs of his sheep – finding them pasture and water, shelter from the weather, and protecting them from wild animals and danger. He watches over them at all times and knows each of them individually.

What did Jesus say about the hired man?

A hired man was paid to look after a flock of sheep. The sheep did not belong to him and he didn't particularly care about them. So when a wolf appeared, the hired man worried more about his own safety and abandoned the flock.

How would you describe a sheep to someone?

White, woolly, bleating. They are timid and gentle animals which like to be kept together with other sheep in a flock. They are not particularly clever and get themselves into all sorts of trouble unless someone is taking care of them.

Do you think Jesus was talking only about sheep?

Jesus is the Good Shepherd and we are his 'flock'. He told this story to make us understand that he cares for us as much as the shepherd cares for his sheep. He watches over us at all times, and knows each of us by name. He goes before us to guide us and keep us from all harm. He takes care of all our needs and we can trust in his goodness.

When Jesus said he would be prepared to give up his life for his flock, what did he mean?

Jesus' love was so strong that he was willing to suffer and die on the cross for our sakes. His sacrifice meant that we can follow him to his heavenly kingdom, where we will share eternal life with him.

ACTIVITY

Using the template given (it will need to be enlarged slightly), cut out some sheep masks from stiff card. Attach these to a stick and help the children to glue cotton wool to the masks.

CLOSING PRAYER

Jesus,
you are the Good Shepherd
and we are your flock.
Help us to know your voice
and always follow you.

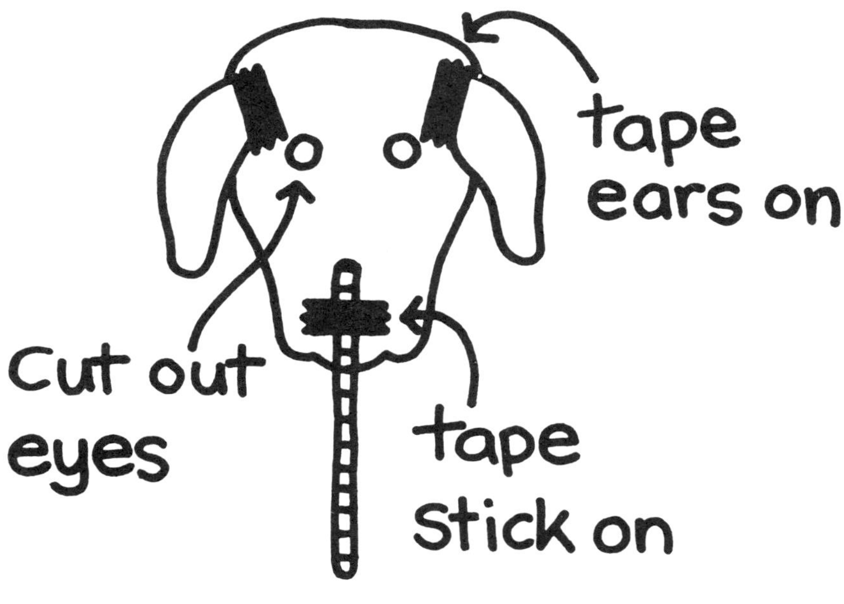
tape
ears on
Cut out
eyes
tape
Stick on

I AM THE WAY

READING

(cf John 14:1-6)

Jesus said to his disciples, 'Do not be afraid or worried, trust in me as you trust in God. In my Father's house there are many rooms, and I am going there to prepare a place for you. Then I shall come back to take you with me, and we will be together again. You already know the way to the place I am going.' Thomas felt unsure and asked Jesus, 'Lord how can we know the way, if we do not know where you are going?' Jesus answered 'I am the way, the truth and the life. Through me you will know how to find my Father's house.'

DISCUSSION

Why did the disciples feel anxious and afraid?

Because Jesus had told them that soon he would be leaving them.

When Jesus talked about going to his Father's house, where do you think he meant?

He was talking about heaven.

Which disciple felt uncertain about what Jesus had told them?

Jesus said that he is 'the way'. Do you know what he meant?

The word 'way' can have several different meanings. Ask one of the children to demonstrate 'the way' to brush their hair or wash their hands – they show us *how to do* something. Then ask another child to explain 'the way' to their house – they tell us *how to find* somewhere. Jesus is 'the way' because he shows us what we must *do* so that we can *find* Heaven.

When we are born we begin our journey through life, following Jesus who shows us the way towards heaven. Our signposts which guide us as we travel are God's commandments and all the things Jesus taught us. If we follow these signposts and *do* what pleases God then we will *find* the right path which leads us to everlasting happiness.

ACTIVITY

Depending on the age range of the group, either get the children to draw around their feet and then cut out the 'footprints', or give out small foot cut-outs to be coloured. These can be used to follow the 'way to Heaven', with signposts which help to show the way. Alternatively the children can draw or print onto the photocopied picture.

CLOSING PRAYER

Before Jesus was born, the people of God used to sing and say prayers and poems called psalms. In this psalm they ask God to 'show them the way'.
(cf Psalm 25:4-5; 8-9)

Teach me your ways Lord.
make them known to me.
Teach me to walk in your truth,
for you are my Saviour
and I can always place my trust in you.
The Lord is just and good.
He shows the humble the way
and teaches them his will.
With loyalty and love
he leads all those who obey his commandments.

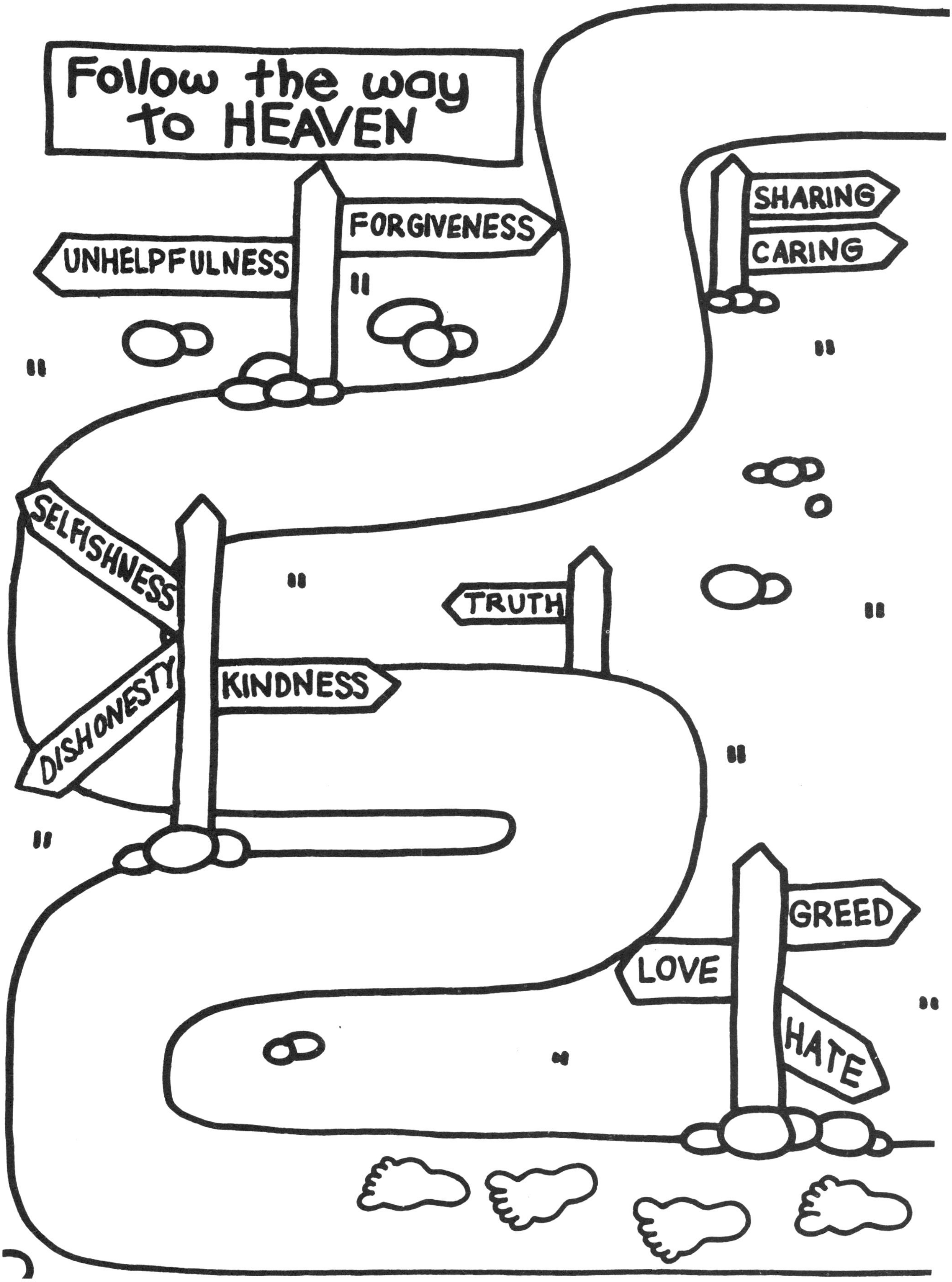

Follow the way to HEAVEN
UNHELPFULNESS
FORGIVENESS
SHARING
CARING
SELFISHNESS
DISHONESTY
KINDNESS
TRUTH
GREED
LOVE
HATE

I WILL NOT LEAVE YOU ON YOUR OWN

Reading

(cf John 14:16-20)

One day, Jesus said to his disciples, 'I will not leave you on your own, I will ask my Father to send you a helper who will stay with you always. The Spirit of God will be with you and in you, though others will not be able to see him or know that he is there. He will fill you with wisdom and understanding. Soon the world will not see me again, but you will know that I am truly alive.'

Discussion

Jesus was going to leave his disciples and return to his heavenly Father.

Whom did he promise to send?

A special helper – the Holy Spirit.

What would this helper look like?

Jesus told them, 'Others will not be able to see him or know that he is there.' The Holy Spirit is one of the great mysteries of God. He is invisible, and one way of describing him is as being like a wind. St John said this about the Holy Spirit: 'The wind blows wherever it pleases; you hear the sound it makes, but you cannot tell where it comes from or where it is going. So it is with the Spirit of God.' *(cf John 3:8)*

Why did Jesus send the Holy Spirit?

Through the Holy Spirit, Jesus remained with the apostles, and he remains with us in the same way today. God sent his Spirit to the apostles to begin the teaching of the Gospel throughout the world. The apostles knew that all the power and strength of their work lay in Jesus. They were useless without him and could not carry on with his work. Through the Holy Spirit he remained with them and his work could continue.

The word 'Spiritus' means breath or wind and that is how we often describe God's Spirit.

If someone asked you to describe the wind, what would you tell them?

- it cannot be seen, but we can see what it does, by making things move, trees bending and leaves blowing around
- we can feel it as it blows against our skin
- it can be very gentle or very powerful

We cannot see the Spirit himself but we can see what he does through the lives of people around us who allow him to guide their words and actions.

If you blew all of the air out of your body and did not breathe any more in, what would happen?

Without breathing you cannot live. The Spirit is the breath of God, who fills us with life and makes us strong.

Activity

Help each child to make a windmill to remind them that wind is one of the forms which the Spirit can take.

Closing Prayer

Come Holy Spirit,
and breathe your life into us,
so that we can bring Christ into the world
and touch the lives of others with his love.

WINDMILL.

1.

Two squares of differently coloured paper.

2.

Stick the two sheets together.

3.

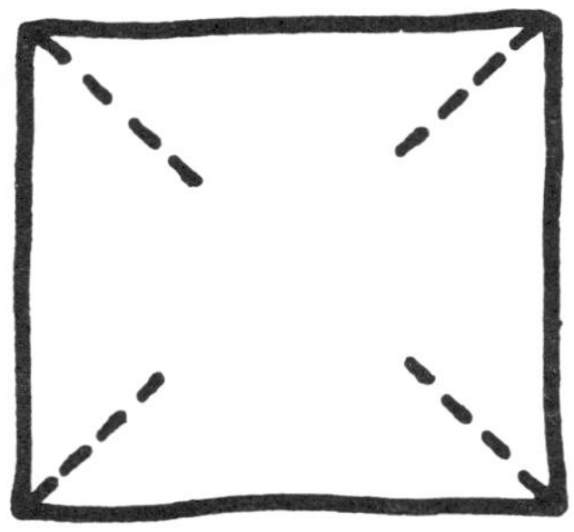

Fold the paper diagonally and cut along the creases halfway to the centre.

4.

Fold every other point into the middle of the square and glue.

5.

Push a butterfly pin through the middle and through a straw.

6.

Open butterfly pin at back of straw.

Blow to make windmill turn.

7.

LOVE EACH OTHER

READING

(cf John 15:9-17)

One day Jesus said to his disciples, 'I love you just as my Father loves me. If you do as I ask then you will always be close to me, and my Father will love you too. I want you to love each other in the same way as I have loved you. There is no greater love than this, that someone should lay down their life for their friends. I have chosen you to be my friends, and am sending you out to share this love with the rest of the world.'

DISCUSSION

What did Jesus ask his disciples to do?

To love one another as he had loved them. Jesus reminded his disciples many times that the greatest commandments were to love God and to love each other.

What does it mean to love another person?

To love someone else means that you care about another person, about their happiness and the things which happen to them. You want only the best for them, and for them to grow in love and goodness.

Jesus' love for us was so great that he did an extraordinary thing for us. What did he do?

He laid down his life for his friends. Jesus loved us so much that he was ready to die so that we could live and share new life with him in heaven. Sometimes in times of disaster, people behave heroically by saving the lives of others instead of their own. Their love for another person is so great that they put that person's needs before their own.

Jesus asked us to share his love with each other. In what ways can we do this?

We can put our love into action:

- by spending some time with someone who is lonely
- by offering help to someone who needs it
- by sharing our happiness with others

Encourage the children to make their own suggestions.

We can put our love into words:

- by telling the members of our family how much we love them
- by praying for the needs of other people
- by praising and thanking God for all that we have

Jesus lives inside each one of us, so whatever we say or do to each other, we say or do it to him. We can make everything we do a little act of love for God.

ACTIVITY

Make a 'love is . . .' booklet for each child with several blank pages for their own drawings and ideas. Either use the illustration here for the cover, or the children can design their own.

Closing Prayer

Heavenly Father,
our hearts are brimming over with your love.
Help us to be generous
and always ready to share this love
with everyone we meet.

Love is...
By

KEEP IN TOUCH

READING

(cf John 17:4-11)

Jesus looked up to heaven and said, 'Father, I have finished the work you sent me to do, and have told my friends all about you. They know that you sent me here, and that through your power, I have been able to do many wonderful things. They have listened to me teaching and they truly believe in you. Father, I pray that you will keep them safe and watch over them always. When I have gone, the world will still be able to see the glory of God through their faith and love.'

DISCUSSION

When Jesus needed to feel very close to his Father, what did he do?

He would pray.

Can you remember some of the times when Jesus prayed?

- in the Garden of Gethsemane, before he was betrayed by Judas
- before he raised Lazarus from the dead
- during the Last Supper, before he broke the bread

Jesus spent a great deal of time praying to his Father. Often he would go off to a quiet place where he would not be disturbed. Like us, Jesus needed to share his worries and problems with his heavenly Father; he knew that he was never alone.

Why is it important for us to pray?

Praying is having a conversation with God. We talk to God and he listens, and then while we listen, God can talk to us too. In this way we get to know God better, we keep in touch.

Do you pray?

When do you pray?

We don't have to have special times for saying prayers. Often we say them at bedtime, but we can talk to God at any time.

Do you ever feel unsure about what to say to God?

God our Father likes to hear about everything we have to tell him, and he is always ready to listen.

The apostles knew how important it was to pray to God, but like us, they often felt uncertain about what to say. One day they asked Jesus to teach them how to pray.

What was the prayer he taught them?

The Lord's Prayer *(Our Father.)*

When we pray it is important to remember several things:

- prayers can be simple thoughts and words coming straight from the heart
- spend a little time with God each day, it doesn't matter where or when
- sometimes God doesn't seem to give us what we pray for. Do not give up praying, keep on talking to God and listening, for he knows what is best for you, even if it is not what you expected
- when we pray, we don't just *ask* God for things we want. Remember to praise and thank him for his goodness, to tell him about ourselves and others and say sorry if we have done wrong
- share your prayers with other people, at school, at home, at church. Jesus said, 'When two or three of you gather together in my name, I'll be there with you.' The Holy Spirit helps us to pray, even if we do not know what to say to God. God will understand us without having to use words

ACTIVITY

Give each child their own copy of the Lord's Prayer to colour and decorate.

CLOSING PRAYER

Together we say the prayer which Jesus himself taught us.
Say the Lord's Prayer, or 'Our Father'.

Our Father who art in Heaven, hallowed be thy name. Thy kingdom come. Thy will be done on earth as it is in heaven.

Give us this day our daily bread and forgive us our trespasses, as we forgive those who trespass against us. And lead us not into temptation, but deliver us from evil.

Amen.

Jesus before Pontius Pilate

Reading

(cf John 18:33-37)

They brought Jesus before Pontius Pilate who asked him, 'Are you the king of the Jews?'

Jesus answered, 'My kingdom is not of this world.'

'So you do indeed claim to be a king!' said Pilate.

'You are the one who calls me king,' answered Jesus. 'I came into this world to share truth and love, and those who know and love the truth will listen to me.'

Discussion

Who was Pontius Pilate?

Pontius Pilate was the Roman governor of Judaea. He was in charge of the Roman army and responsible for keeping the peace. He acted as judge when serious crimes were committed.

Why was Jesus brought before Pontius Pilate?

The Jewish leaders had seen the welcome given to Jesus as he entered Jerusalem, and they were afraid of his position and power. They wanted to get rid of Jesus by whatever means they could, so they took Jesus to Pilate and asked for him to be sentenced to death.

What question did Pontius Pilate ask Jesus?

Jesus tried to explain that he was not a king who belonged to this world, but that he had come into the world to share his kingdom of love and goodness.

Did Pilate listen to Jesus and understand what he had said?

Pilate knew that Jesus was harmless and had done nothing wrong, but he was more interested in keeping the peace and not upsetting the Jewish leaders, than in seeing that justice was done. He allowed the Jewish leaders to have their own way, and eventually handed Jesus over to be put to death.

What happened after Jesus had suffered and died on the cross?

Three days later, on Easter Sunday, he rose from the dead and showed the world that he is the king of the universe, with the power to conquer death and bring new and everlasting life.

Activity

Cut out crown shapes from card and write on each one 'Christ is our King'. Decorate these and staple the crowns so that they can be worn or carried by the children.

Closing Prayer

God our Father
we thank you
for sending your only Son to be our saviour.
Help us to know and love your truth
and to listen to you always.

1. Cut out crown shapes from stiff card.

2. Decorate with stick-on-shapes and glitter.

3. Staple crowns two ends together.

4.

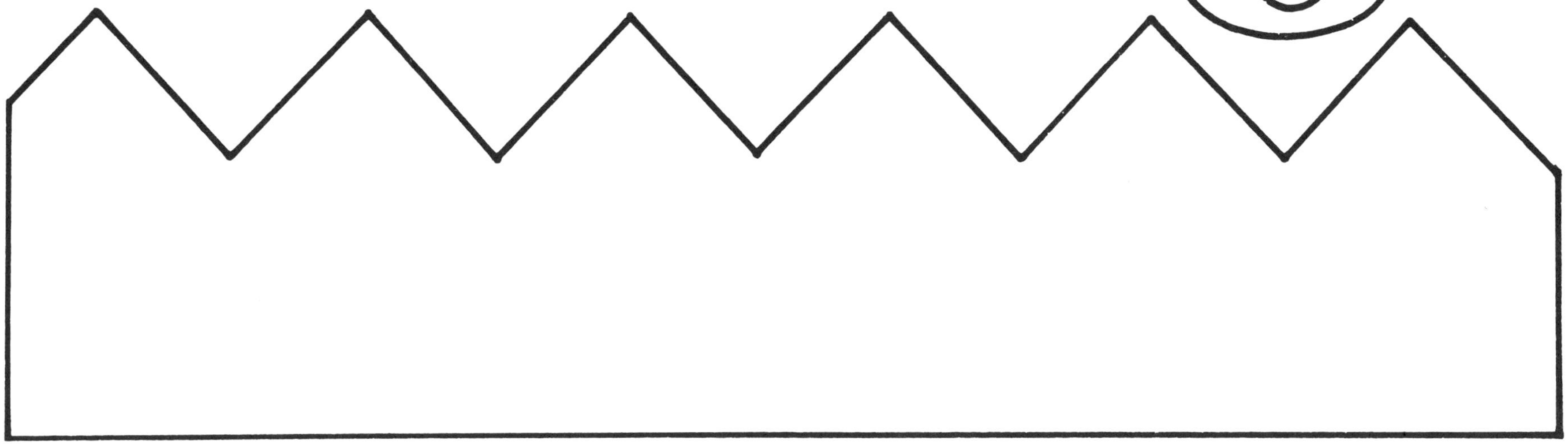

DOUBTING THOMAS

READING

(cf John 20:19-29)

On the Sunday after Jesus had died, his disciples sat huddled together in a locked room, hidden away for fear of being arrested. Suddenly Jesus appeared in the room with them. 'Peace be with you,' he said and he showed them the wounds in his hands and his side. His disciples were overjoyed to see their master again. 'As my father sent me, so I am sending you,' he said. Then breathing on them he said, 'Receive the Holy Spirit, and know that whoever you forgive, I will forgive also!'

The disciple called Thomas was not with the others when Jesus had appeared, and because he had not seen him with his own eyes, he did not believe that Jesus was alive.

A week later Jesus appeared to them again and, greeted them with the words, 'Peace be with you.' He showed his wounds to Thomas and said, 'Doubt no longer, Thomas.' At once Thomas fell to his knees and cried, 'My Lord and my God.'

Jesus said to him, 'You believe because you have seen me with your own eyes. Blessed are those who have not seen and yet believe.'

DISCUSSION

When Jesus first appeared to the disciples in the locked room, which one of them was missing?

Thomas was not with the other disciples, and the Gospel does not explain where he was.

What did Jesus do when he appeared?

He shared the gift of his peace saying the words, 'Peace be with you'. Then he gave them the gift of the Holy Spirit to increase their faith and courage.

Did Thomas believe the disciples when they told him that Jesus had risen from the dead?

Thomas could not believe without seeing.

When Jesus appeared again he showed Thomas his wounds. Was he angry because Thomas had doubted?

Because Thomas could see and touch Jesus, he believed that he had risen from the dead. Jesus understood that many like Thomas would hear the story of the resurrection and be filled with doubt.

Can we 'see' the risen Jesus today?

Jesus lives amongst us and we can recognise his presence in the people around us. A kind action or a loving remark are signs of Christ's power working through other people.

What words did Thomas say when he recognised Jesus as the risen Lord?

'My Lord and my God'.

We cannot see Jesus but we *believe* that he is alive and present with us.

ACTIVITY

Cut out the shape of a large cross from a piece of stiff card and either paint it black or cover it with black or dark paper. Prepare small squares of coloured tissue paper, to make 'flowers'. Stick some of these onto the cross, while older children string others together to make a garland to hang on the cross. The 'Resurrection cross' can be attached to a stand or hung as a mobile. Add the caption: 'We believe Jesus is risen'.

CLOSING PRAYER

Today we pray for those like Thomas,
who cannot believe without seeing.
Increase their faith Lord,
and help them to recognise you
in the people they meet everyday.

Tissue paper
1.
2.
Twist in middle and attach with sticky tape.
3.
Thread flowers onto string
4.
garland
Tissue paper flower
We believe Jesus is risen
garland
Tissue paper flowers

Breakfast on the Shore

Gospel

(cf John 21:1-17)

Peter and some of the disciples had been fishing all night but had caught nothing. As daylight dawned, they noticed a man on the shore who called out to them, 'Have you caught anything?'

As they shook their heads, the stranger said, 'Try once more over there!'

They threw their nets back into the water and caught so many fish that their nets were ready to burst. At that moment Peter recognised Jesus, and jumping into the water, he swam to meet him.

On the beach, Jesus had made a fire and was cooking breakfast for Peter and his friends. After they had eaten, Jesus turned to Peter and asked, 'Do you love me?'

'Yes, Lord, you know that I love you,' Peter said.

Jesus asked Peter this question three times and after he had answered, Jesus told Peter about the work he wanted him to do.

Discussion

What made Peter recognise Jesus that day?

Jesus told Peter and the other disciples to cast their nets again, and suddenly they found them full of fish. Peter knew that only the Son of God had the power to work such a miracle.

When the disciples found Jesus on the shore, what was he doing?

Jesus was preparing breakfast for them as a sign of his love and friendship. He wanted to share a meal with his friends, just as he had done many times before, to prove to them that he was truly alive.

Have you ever prepared a meal for a special occasion to show how much you cared for someone?

Perhaps you have helped to bake a birthday cake, or brought breakfast in bed for one of your family.

When they had finished eating, what did Jesus ask Peter?

Jesus asked Peter the same question three times, 'Do you love me?' Each time Peter answered, 'Yes, Lord, you know I love you.'

Why do you think Jesus might have asked this on three occasions?

When Jesus was arrested, Peter was asked three times whether he was a friend of Jesus, and each time he said, 'No'. Jesus gave Peter another chance to prove his love for him. He wanted Peter to know that he trusted in his love, and wanted Peter to share this love and faith with the rest of the world.

Activity

Help the children to re-tell today's Gospel story in their own words and to imagine the scene. Ask them to draw a picture of Jesus preparing breakfast for his friends that morning on the shore.

Alternatively they can rewrite the story in a mini-book using the picture strip drawings.

Closing Prayer

Lord Jesus,
help us to recognise you
in the world around us
and to show how much we love you
by our words and actions.

JESUS ON THE SHORE

WE BELONG TO ONE BODY

READING

(cf 1 Cor 12:12-30)

Just as your body has many different parts, so it is with the Christian family. Each part of your body has a special job to do, and without that part, your body could not work properly. Without your legs you could not stand up and walk. Many different parts make up one body, and every part is just as important as another. Each one of us belongs to the one family of God, and has special gifts which God has given to us. We must use these gifts to make sure that the one body of Christ works properly and is full of life.

DISCUSSION

Ask the children to point to each part of their body as you read this list: head, toes, elbow, mouth, knee, nose, back, ear.

Which one of these parts is most important?

Each part of the body does its own particular job, which only it can do. You cannot see with your ears, nor smell with your knees! The whole body relies on the eyes for sight, and on the ears to hear, and on the legs to carry it about. No part can manage without the others, and they are all equally important.

St Paul compared us to parts of the one body of Christ. What did he mean?

Each of us is a member of the family of God and we are invited to share in the life of Jesus who rose from the dead. Although there are many Christians in the world today, together we make up one Church, or one body which believes in and follows the teachings of Jesus.

As many parts belonging to the one body of Christ, what jobs can we do in the Church and in our ordinary lives?

We can put whatever talents we have to good use in lots of different ways. Many people help us to celebrate at church on Sunday – the musicians and choir, the flower arrangers, the readers, the people who welcome us at the door. They do all these jobs on behalf of everyone. In the same way, in our ordinary lives, our acts of kindness and love work on behalf of everyone else who belongs to the family of God.

ACTIVITY

Cut out the various parts of the body as illustrated. Punch holes in the relevant places (take care if you are doing this with the children) and ask the children to assemble a body from the various parts using butterfly pins!

CLOSING PRAYER

Lord Jesus,
you call each one of us
to belong to one people,
the family of God.
Help us,
together with our brothers and sisters,
to share your love
with the world.